The Marvelous Macadamia Nut

Rabbit Island from Waimanalo Beach on Oahu

by Rebecca Buyers

with Helen Caivano, Catherine Johnson and Joann Carroll Linden

Illustrations by Marc Rosenthal

IRENA CHALMERS COOKBOOKS INC.

New York

To my father,
John William Amerman Buyers

IRENA CHALMERS COOKBOOKS INC.

23 East 92nd Street
New York, NY 10028
(212) 289-3105

PUBLISHER
Irena Chalmers

Managing Editor
Jean Atcheson

Book Design
Milton Glaser
Karen Skelton, *Associate Designer*

ISBN 0-941034-74-7
©' 1982 by Rebecca W. Buyers-Basso. All rights reserved.
Printed and published in the United States of America
by Irena Chalmers Cookbooks, Inc.
LIBRARY OF CONGRESS
CATALOG CARD NO.: 82-073616

   Buyers, Rebecca
      The marvelous macadamia nut.

New York, NY: Chalmers, Irena, Cookbooks, Inc.
84p.

EDCBA 65432

Full Grown Macadamia

Contents

Introduction	8
A History of the Macadamia Nut	9
About Cooking with Macadamias	16
Cakes and Tortes	18
Sugar Crumb Tea Cake	20
Macadamia Topping	20
Cardamom Spice Coffee Cake	21
Spicy Applesauce Cake	22
Vanilla Buttercream Icing	22
Macadamia Orange Tea Cake	23
Citrus-Glazed Sour Cream Cake	24
German Chocolate Cake Macadamia	26
Coconut Macadamia Filling	26
Cinnamon Nut Flan	28
Macadamia Nut Torte	28
Pineapple Blitz Torte	29
Pineapple Filling	29
Lemon Macadamia Torte	30
Lemon Filling	30
Chocolate Lovers' Nut Torte	32
Mocha Icing	32
Kiwi Coconut Cake	33
Kiwi Filling and Icing	33
Blueberry Nut Cake	34
Pineapple Carrot Cake Macadamia	34
Pineapple Cream Cheese Filling	34
Tropical Upside Down Cake	35
Carrot Cake	35
Cardamom Wedding Torte	36
Orange Buttercream Filling	36

Orange Nut Cake	37
Orange Icing	37
Pies	38
Strawberry Cheese Pie	40
Pastry Shell	40
Lenore's Cheese Pie	41
Graham Cracker Crumb-Nut Crust	41
Orange Yogurt Cream Cheese Pie	42
Unbaked Graham Cracker Honey-Nut Crust	42
Macadamia Lemon-Rum Chiffon Pie	43
Butter Crust	43
Macadamia Coconut Pie	44
Sour Cream Apple Pie ('Awa Kalima Apala Pai)	44
Hawaiian Apple Pie	46
Macadamia Pie Crust	46
Strawberry Rhubarb Pie (Ohelo-Papa Rhubarb Pai)	47
Banana Pukini Pai	47
Blueberry Cream Pie	48
Macadamia Nut Crust	48
Meg's Macadamia Nut Pie	48
Macadamia Pineapple Cream Pie	49
Cookies and Bars	50
Macadamia Nut Meringue Cookies	52
Macadamia Macaroons	52
Macadamia Walnut Meringues	53
Coconut Macaroons	53

Macadamia Lace Cookies	54
Macadamia Cream Cookies	54
Basque Nut Cookies	55
Snowballs	55
Chocolate-Topped Macadamia Nut Cookies	56
Chocolate Topping	56
Frozen Chocolate Macadamia Nut Squares	58
Coconut Chews	58
Cinnamon Squares	59
Macadamia Nut-Rum Bars	59
Lemon-Coconut-Nut Squares	60
Lemon Frosting	60
Fruit-Filled Bars	61
Margot's Brownies	61
Cream Cheese Swirl Brownies	62
Carole's Blondies	62
Mauna Loa Brownies	63

Desserts — 64

Hawaiian Fruit Cup	66
Tropical Compote	66
Tropical Fruits Mauna Loa	67
Mango Cream	67
Hot Apple Crunch	68
Sugar Plum Pudding	68
Cathy's Crepe Batter	70
Macadamia Nut Filling	70
Mocha Sauce	70
Linzertorte	71
Chocolate Mousse	71
Macadamia Chocolate Mousse Pie	72
Rolled Macadamia Coconut Baklava	73
Ricotta-Macadamia Strudel	74
Lemon Soufflé	76
Maple Macadamia Soufflé	76

Date Soufflé	77
Prune Nut Soufflé	77

Candies and Ice Cream — 78

Spiced Macadamias	80
Macadamia Nougat	80
Macadamian Date Balls	80
Creamy Nut Fudge	81
Macadamia Nut Clusters	81
Caramel Crunch Ice Cream	82
Chocolate Candy Pie Crust	83
Mint Ice Cream	83
Skip's Macadamia Ice Cream Sauce	83
Hawaiian Rainbow Bombe	84

Hibiscus Blossom

Acknowledgments

The Marvelous Macadamia Nut would not have been possible without the help and encouragement of many people. First, I must thank my father for offering me the opportunity to create this book, and my husband, Skip, for his unshakable confidence in my ability to tackle such an ambitious project.

The names of my co-authors—Helen Caivano, Catherine Johnson and Joann Carroll Linden—rightfully belong on the front cover with mine. They shared equally in the work of recipe development, cook-testing and selection from the literally hundreds of recipes we accumulated. Each one of them contributed her time, energy and imagination without reserve through the many months it took to turn the idea of a macadamia dessert cookbook into reality, and I cannot thank them enough for their help.

While Joann and I were on the Big Island of Hawaii, during the research phase of this project, we enjoyed the gracious hospitality of Paul Bennett, President of the Mauna Loa Macadamia Nut Corporation, and his wife, Diane. And during a visit to the Mauna Loa orchards at Keaau, we learned more in one afternoon about how macadamia nuts are grown and processed than most people learn in a lifetime. We thank Nina Ann Akahoshi and Alan Yamaguchi for their time, their knowledge and their Island friendliness.

Special thanks go, too, to all the people at the Mauna Loa headquarters in Honolulu who helped us with our research: in particular, to Betsy Sandstrom, who supplied us with information on the history of the macadamia nut industry, and opened file after file of news clippings and recipes, and to Ian Killips, who contributed many valuable ideas for the book's cover and contents.

I am very grateful to Anita Fial, of Lewis and Neale, Inc., of New York, who was responsible for bringing our embryonic cookbook to the attention of Irena Chalmers. Irena, and Jean Atcheson, our editor, are women with extraordinary energy and expertise. It has been a joy and an education to work with them.

We are indebted to the following for submitting their original recipes to us for conversion to macadamia fare: Skip Basso, Carole Beal, Carey Bell, Carol Case, Meg Caivano, Irena Chalmers, Martha Collet, Barbara Grey, Paul Heroux, Lindsey Linden, Margot McGregor, Jean Johnson and Mary Ann Viola. On a more personal note, I'd like to thank my Grandma Buyers for teaching me to appreciate good food and for showing me the fundamentals of cooking, and Dennis Gilbert and Amy Bens for interesting me in cooking as an art form.

Finally, our thanks to all the people whose encouragement kept us enthusiastic about macadamia nuts through the long cold winter of test-cooking in Bar Harbor, Maine and Philadelphia, so many thousands of miles from the sunny Hawaiian

Islands: my mother, Elsie Buyers, and my sisters, Ellie and Janey; our spouses, Skip Basso, Roc Caivano, Sam Eliot and Lindsey Linden; Marcia Dvorak and Ann Outzen, George Demas, George Benington, Catherine Luyster, Kari Koss, Dana Friis-Hansen, Cynthia Chisholm, Karen Fromm Russell and Rachelle Minkoff. Each did or said the right thing at a critical time when work appeared to be overwhelming. Their faith in us made all the difference.

Aloha Nui Loa,

Rebecca W. Buyers

Macadamia Nuts
on the Tree

Introduction

Macadamia nuts are *special*. On this point it is difficult to argue. But what makes them so special? They can easily be described in terms of other nuts. They resemble hazelnuts (filberts) in shape and Brazil nuts in color. They grow on trees, like chestnuts, in the tropics, like cashews, to about the size of walnuts. They are as rich as pecans, as addictive as peanuts and as versatile as almonds. However, when it comes to describing the taste of macadamia nuts, there is no comparison. They have a buttery sweet and slightly salty flavor with a delicate texture that sets them apart from all other nuts. But their unique taste is only part of what makes macadamia nuts so special.

Macadamia nuts are also *exotic*. Generally associated with Hawaii, where 90 percent of the commercial macadamia nut crop is now grown, they are actually indigenous to the coastal rain forests of northeastern Australia. In addition to Hawaii, they are also grown on a smaller scale in various parts of Africa, Latin America and Australia, and experimentally in California and Florida.

Macadamia nuts are *new*. Relatively speaking, the macadamia has a very short history in the modern world. Although the nuts were a staple of Australian aborigines for hundreds of years (nobody really knows how long), the edible species of macadamia was not discovered by Europeans until 1859, and the nuts were not sold commercially until 1934. They have only become popular in the past 20 years as a direct result of the increase in tourism to the Hawaiian Islands.

Macadamia nuts are *rare*. They are one of the most expensive nut meats on the market, yet the demand for them is so great that the macadamia industry's biggest problem has been to produce nuts in sufficient quantities to satisfy would-be buyers. For a number of technical and scientific reasons the macadamia is difficult to grow, and this has kept production down. However, with the recent decrease in demand for sugar cane, one of Hawaii's major crops, many acres of unprofitable cane land are being converted to macadamia nut orchards. (This is particularly good news for mainlanders who have had trouble finding macadamia nuts in sufficient supply.)

Macadamia nuts are *delicious* as an ingredient in baking and candy-making, and although such a use might seem outrageously extravagant, it isn't really. Nut bits are considerably less expensive than whole macadamias, and for most baking purposes the bits are best. Hawaiians have known both these facts for a long time; fortunately, nut bits are also becoming increasingly available in the continental United States in supermarkets and specialty stores as well as fine food shops.

This book has been designed for everyone who would like to recreate a taste of Hawaii. Marc Rosenthal's superb watercolors illustrate some of the stages in the growing of macadamias and evoke the interplay of light and color that makes the islands memorable. As for the recipes, some are from Island families who have shared their heritage with us; a few are adaptations from recipes originally made with other nuts; most have sprung directly from our own experience and imagination. We collected everything we could find using macadamias, divided the sections between us and tested each recipe again and again until we were ready to check each other's findings. In the process we rejected many times more recipes than we have included. The 75 recipes that follow we genuinely believe are all well worth trying — they looked good and tasted good when we made them. May they delight you, too!

A History of the Macadamia Nut

The history of the macadamia nut begins in the isolated tropical and subtropical rain forests of Australia, long before that continent was discovered by European explorers, at a time when there were only about 300,000 aborigines inhabiting the land. These native people, who lived simply and in harmony with the wilderness, ate turtle eggs, fish, shellfish, kangaroo, koala, wombat and bandicoot meat, small birds, the grubs of certain treeback insects, yams and grass seeds. At the same time each year, however, during the fall and early winter, these people would congregate on the eastern slopes of Australia's Great Dividing Range, to gather and feast on the seeds of two evergreen trees, one of which they called the "Kindal-Kindal." (Botanists have since identified this as the edible macadamia nut and given it the name *Macadamia integrifolia.*)

About 1857, the macadamia nut tree was formally "discovered" by a British botanist named Ferdinand von Mueller and Walter Hill, the director of the botanical gardens of Brisbane, Australia. The two men were struck with the majestic beauty of the specimens they found growing in the rain forests of Queensland. The tree then became designated scientifically as *Macadamia ternifolia,* a new member of the family Proteaceae. The genus Macadamia was named after John Macadam, a prominent scientist who was at that time serving as secretary of the Philosophical Institute of Victoria, Australia.

Dr. Macadam is often credited with being the first European to recognize the edible quality of the macadamia nut. However, W.B. Storey, author of *History of the Macadamia Nut* (1977), gives the credit to an anonymous teenage boy, who was one of Walter Hill's assistants. According to Storey's story, Hill gave the boy a bag of nuts from the newly discovered macadamia trees and told him to husk them so that they could be planted in the gardens. When the boy returned the husked nuts to Hill, the botanist noticed that several were missing. When questioned about their whereabouts, the boy admitted to having snitched a few because he found them very good eating. Hill was incredulous because he had tasted the nuts of what he thought were the same genus of macadamia on an earlier botanical expedition, and had found them bitter and inedible. The boy insisted, however, that the nuts were quite tasty and convinced Hill to give them a second chance—which the baffled botanist did, and found them much to his liking!

Shortly thereafter, a distinction was made between macadamia nut trees with edible nuts, *Macadamia integrifolia* or smooth-shelled macadamias, and those with bitter nuts, *Macadamia ternifolia* or rough-shelled nuts—"gympie nuts," as they later became known in Australia. (There was still some confusion, however, because there is also a rough-shelled species, *Macadamia tetraphylla,* which produces a nut that is edible—though not as good eating as *integrifolia*— and to compound the identification problem, seedlings from the same parent macadamia frequently produce nuts of very different quality.)

The first macadamia nuts to reach the shores of the Hawaiian Islands from Australia traveled by steamship as the precious cargo of a Mr. William H. Purvis. That was sometime between 1878 and 1881 (no two accounts give the same year) and Mr. Purvis was returning home to his sugar plantation at Honokua on the Big Island with some gympie nut seeds to plant in his gardens. He too had admired the trees for their beauty and ornamental value.

Macadamia trees *are* very beautiful. They grow slowly and live for 50 years or more, spreading majestically from heights of 40 and 50 feet. They have shiny green hollylike leaves and bear sprays of long, delicate, sweet-smelling white blossoms. Each spray of 40 or 50 flowers produces from four to eight "nutlets," which will eventually ripen into nuts. The nuts themselves grow encased in a very hard, woody shell, which is protected by a thick and fibrous green husk, not unlike the husk of a chestnut. In its natural state, a tree will have flowers, nutlets and fully mature nuts growing simultaneously in riotous profusion all year round, although the commercial growers have succeeded in shortening the harvest period to four or five months a year.

Purvis planted several of these trees on his Honokua property and they grew very well. But visitors to his home, who sampled the nuts borne by the new trees, declared their taste to be "slightly bitter" and not for eating. This variety of macadamia continued to be cultivated in Hawaii for the next 40 years by those who, like Purvis, valued the tree entirely for its beauty.

In the same period, however, the more palatable, smooth-shelled macadamia was introduced to the islands from Queensland by two brothers, R.A. and E.W. Jordan, who started a small nursery of seedlings in Honolulu. It was from those original seedlings that all the subsequent major plantings in Hawaii were made.

Of course, it was a long process, and the macadamias we eat today are the end result of commercial breeding toward the best possible qualities—lightness of color, texture, ability to withstand disease, strength of the root stock and so on. The more I learn about the story behind the nuts, the more I come to appreciate the uniqueness of their flavor and the vulnerability of the trees' health.

Industry development of the macadamia in Hawaii came about through the concerted efforts of the territorial government, the Agricultural Experiment Station of the University of Hawaii, and the entrepreneurial vision of private investors. For example, as early as 1892, the government Board of Agriculture and Forestry planted rough-shelled macadamia seedlings on the top of Mt. Tantalus, on Oahu, as part of a reforestation project. Less than 20 years later, J.E. Higgins, a horticulturalist at the Agricultural Experiment Station, distributed macadamia seedlings to coffee growers on the Kona Coast of Hawaii, hoping to supplement farmers' incomes at a time when coffee prices were low. (When coffee prices rose, however, interest in the new crop declined.)

Blossoms and young nuts

It was Ernest Shelton Van Tassel, a private businessman, who really pioneered the macadamia nut as a cash crop. Crippled by an attack of polio in midlife, Van Tassel left his home in Wellesley, Massachusetts and traveled to Hawaii in the hope of regaining his health. There he met some beach boys who encouraged him to swim in the ocean for therapy. The practice seemed to him to alleviate his paralysis, although he still had to use two walking sticks, and he decided to make the islands his home.

Soon after his arrival in 1916, Van Tassel made the acquaintance of home-roasted macadamia nuts, often served in fashionable Hawaiian homes, and he recognized the commercial potential of the nut. In 1921 he had his first orchard planted. Unfortunately, he knew more about business than horticulture. The seedlings were put into the ground still encased in the tin cans in which they had been germinated, and inevitably, every one of them died. Van Tassel learned a valuable lesson from his disaster: if he were going to get anywhere in this business, he needed an experienced horticulturist at his side.

In the course of the next decade, Van Tassel organized a stock company called the Hawaiian Macadamia Nut Company to bankroll a second planting of 2,500 seedlings (this time without the tin cans), and hired a horticulturist who knew about macadamias. Ralph Moltzau had worked as a summer employee for the Hawaii Agricultural Experiment Station while he was still a schoolboy. In 1926, he had successfully grafted together two different species of macadamias, a feat which most horticulturalists of the time had thought was impossible. Moltzau was definitely Van Tassel's man.

By 1933, Van Tassel was raising enough macadamia nuts to make it worth building a processing plant in the Kakaako section of Honolulu, and in 1934 shoppers in Hawaii saw a new product on the shelves in retail stores—"Van's Macadamia Nuts." The undaunted Van Tassel extended the market for his nuts as far afield as the West Coast as well, before he died in 1943 and the Hawaiian Macadamia Nut Company lost its motivating force. By this time, however, large companies with ample financial resources had become interested in the potential of the macadamia industry.

When Van Tassel and Ralph Moltzau were just starting up, the legislature of the territory of Hawaii passed an act exempting all lands used solely for macadamia nut culture from taxation for a period of five years. This stimulus prompted Walter P. Naquin, manager of the Honokoa Sugar Company, to convert some 450 acres of unprofitable sugar cane land to growing macadamias. Meanwhile, J.W. Beaumont, a horticulturist at the University of Hawaii, enlisted Ralph Moltzau's help in embarking on a systematic program of experimentation to find the very best trees among the 60,000 seedlings then growing in the territory, and propagate them by cloning.

This program was much more complicated than it sounds, because the thousands of seedlings were growing, not in one large orchard, where examining them would have been easy, but scattered about the islands in 10-acre plots. Many of the small plantings were on sugar plantations, and each individual variety, in consequence, would be named for that orchard.

I met a man on my last visit to Hawaii who had grown up on a sugar plantation in the Aiea district of Honolulu (where the airport now is) and remembered that there had been a 10-acre macadamia plot on the place during the 1930s. As a boy, he said, he used to collect the nuts as they ripened and then go to great efforts to crack them open (macadamia nuts are notoriously hard to break). He would take the nut meats to the family cook for her to sauté in a little salted butter. He said he would watch them greedily while they cooled and then eat them *immediately,* before anybody else in the family smelled the special treat.

While this man was enjoying a carefree boyhood, Beaumont's ambitious project

A New Graft

was paying off in new methods. In 1937, he was able to report the success of "girding" branches from which "scions" (smaller branches to be grafted to a different root stock) would be taken, one month in advance of their use as grafts. He discovered that such girding causes starch to accumulate above the girdle, which the scion can then use as food until it is well established with the stock. The following year, Beaumont and Moltzau co-authored a manual entitled *Nursing, Propagation and Topworking of the Macadamia* and two other bulletins on seedlings and processing. In 1939, ten 10-acre plantings were made with cooperative growers on Kauai, Oahu, Maui and the Big Island to evaluate the selections Beaumont and Moltzau had made from the 60,000 seedlings. Macadamia growing was about to become a business.

In 1940, Naquin's Honokoa Sugar Company built a macadamia nut processing factory at Haina, on the Big Island; macadamia nut seedlings were planted experimentally in California; Beaumont became director of the Hawaii Agricultural Experiment Station; and Moltzau took over the direction of operations at the Hawaiian Macadamia Nut Company. (That business was later acquired by Theo H. Davies and Co., who used the brand name "Hawaiian Holiday," and in 1974, Davies sold the operation to San Francisco entrepreneur Paul De Domenico, who continues to run it very successfully.)

The macadamia nut industry was well established in Hawaii by the late 1940s, when Castle & Cooke, the owners of Dole Pineapple, bought 1,000 acres at Keaau on the Big Island. Using bulldozers, they cleared an area of dense tropical rain forest which proved ideal for growing macadamias—it experienced the proper amount of rainfall, had good soil drainage, enjoyed moderate temperature fluctuations and wasn't too windy. On January 4, 1949, the first macadamia nut tree was planted in the Keaau orchard. Eventually 1,100 acres were planted and a processing factory was built right on the site. By 1955, commercial nuts were being produced under the brand name "Royal Hawaiian Macadamia Nuts."

C. Brewer and Co., Ltd., the oldest company in Hawaii, had been involved primarily in sugar production until the 1950s, when the firm began looking for a crop that could be cultivated on land that was marginal for sugar cane. Like Honokoa Sugar, Brewer turned to macadamias, and the first tree was planted in 1961 in the Ka'u district on the Big Island. In 1974, Brewer bought the Keaau macadamia orchards from Castle & Cooke, renamed them the Brewer Orchards —and became the largest producer of macadamia nuts in the world.

Today macadamia nuts remain by far the costliest nut in the world to produce. Once the grafting process has taken place, the trees have to be carefully tended in a nursery for a couple of years until they are strong enough to stand in the rough lava earth. After they are transplanted to an orchard, it is another five years before they begin to bear. It takes 15 years in all for a tree to reach full production. In addition, each tree requires not one, but five to six harvests annually. The mature nuts, of course, fall to the ground, but so do the dead leaves, which have to be blown from the area before the nuts can be harvested.

Once gathered, the nuts have to be dehusked, then dried and cured to reduce the moisture so that the kernel can be separated, undamaged, from the woody shell. It takes 330 pounds per square inch of pressure to break a macadamia nut's shell. In the old precommercial days, the nuts used to be put between wooden boards and automobiles were driven over the top to crack them, after which everybody scrambled to collect the nuts and bits. One modern method is to pass the nuts between counter-rotating steel rollers, precisely spaced to crack the shell without disturbing the kernel.

Next, the nuts are color-sorted electronically for light, uniform color, then roasted in high-grade coconut oil, then sorted again. Only fancy grade nuts are lightly salted and packed for retail distribution. Any that are not uniform are set aside for other uses, such as making nut brittle and ice cream.

All told, there are more than 13,700 acres of macadamia orchards currently growing in Hawaii. But even with many sections of cane land being converted to macadamia production, it will be a long time before macadamia nut supply catches up to world demand. It is also possible that with more people every year tasting the marvelous nut for the first time, falling in love with it, and demanding more—it never will.

Sorting Nuts

About Cooking with Macadamias

The macadamia nut contains a high percentage of polyunsaturated vegetable oil (about 78 percent) and a low percentage of moisture (1.5 percent). It is a good source of calcium, phosphorus, iron and vitamin B 1. Half an ounce equals 100 calories.

Once a macadamia container is opened, it is important to refrigerate it—unless, as so often happens, it is emptied at first sitting!

Macadamia nut bits are a natural way to enjoy macadamias. Because the nut shells are so extremely hard, making it difficult to extract the nuts whole, they have been eaten in pieces ever since the Australian aborigines first pounded them with rocks to crack them. In the early days of macadamia growing in Hawaii, the islanders cracked the nuts with hammers or crushed them beneath the wheels of their automobiles. Whatever pieces emerged from all this activity were often sauteed in butter and eaten when cooled. In the modern processing, both the whole nuts and the bits are roasted in coconut oil, but unlike the whole nuts, the bits are sold unsalted.

Cooking with macadamia nut bits is ideal because they *are* unsalted, so you do not have to readjust the amount of salt when using your own recipes. When you are making an uncooked candy, cookie or pie filling, the bits will benefit from being roasted to bring out their full flavor. To roast them, preheat the oven to 300 degrees, spread the measured amount of bits on a cookie sheet and cook for about 3 or 4 minutes, until lightly browned. Watch them closely and be careful not to burn them.

Macadamia nut bits are not yet available everywhere. If you can't find them, chop the whole nuts into splinters and measure the amount for your needs. Be sure to adjust the amount of salt in the recipe, however, as the whole nuts are only available salted, unless they are being purchased in bulk.

About the Recipes

All the recipes were tested with white, unsifted all-purpose flour. Sugar, unless otherwise specified, means white granulated sugar. When brown sugar was needed, we used light brown sugar in all our testing. (Be sure to pack it firmly when measuring.) The butter is unsalted butter. We used whole milk and medium-sized eggs. Regarding spices, it is best to use freshly ground nutmeg, cloves, cinnamon and cardamom for full flavor, and there is no substitute for real vanilla. We used

Grand Marnier where recipes specify orange liqueur and Kahlua for coffee liqueur.

In recipes calling for honey, we used Mauna Loa macadamia honey, which is made by the same bees that pollinate the delicate macadamia blossoms. The bees are brought into the orchard during the trees' most active period, specifically for that purpose. The strong, sweet honey is a delicious by-product of this natural relationship between the trees and the bees.

The easiest recipes are unmarked; they take little time and are ideal for a quick snack or an impromptu party. Those with ✳ are more difficult or time-consuming; those marked ✳✳ are either quite tricky or really do take time to prepare. They are well worth the effort involved, however, so plan ahead for these or save them for really special occasions.

Happy baking! Happy eating!

Young trees in the Nursery

17

Cakes and Tortes

As far as we can tell, the difference between a cake and a torte is flour. A cake uses flour and a torte uses ground nuts and/or breadcrumbs (though some may use a little flour in addition).

Macadamia nuts lend themselves beautifully to both cakes and tortes. They have a delicate yet distinct flavor which enhances even the most basic ingredients. We found the combination of macadamia nuts and citrus fruit to be especially good. The moist, tangy Macadamia Orange Tea Cake, for example, is a particular favorite of ours, as is the Lemon Macadamia Torte, with a filling that resembles luscious lemon custard, while the intense citrus flavor of the Orange Nut Cake actually seems to bring forward the taste of the nuts. Don't miss making the Kiwi Coconut Cake, either, for the sheer pleasure of creating its interlaced topping of pale green kiwi fruit, interspersed with puffs of cream surmounted by golden nuts.

This section is loosely divided into three sections—tea cakes, dessert cakes and rich dessert tortes. Of course, anyone would be happy to have a torte at lunch or a tea cake at midnight, so don't be constrained by our groupings.

A Lush Island Valley

Sugar Crumb Tea Cake

2 cups flour, sifted
1½ cups sugar
½ teaspoon cinnamon
¼ teaspoon nutmeg
8 tablespoons (1 stick) butter,
  softened
½ cup macadamia nut bits
1 teaspoon baking soda
¼ teaspoon salt
1 cup sour cream
1 egg, beaten

½ cup macadamia nut bits
2 tablespoons sugar
½ teaspoon cinnamon
¼ teaspoon nutmeg

Preheat the oven to 350 degrees. Grease a 9-inch-square baking pan.

Sift the flour, sugar, cinnamon and nutmeg into a mixing bowl. Cut in the butter until the mixture resembles fine breadcrumbs. Mix half the crumb mixture with the macadamias and press over the bottom of the baking pan.

Stir the baking soda and salt into the sour cream, add to the remaining crumbs along with the beaten egg and mix thoroughly. Spread the batter evenly over the crumbs in the pan. Sprinkle the top evenly with Macadamia Topping (below).

Bake in the preheated oven for about 40 minutes, or until a cake tester inserted into the center comes out clean. Cut into squares and serve warm.

Macadamia Topping

Mix all the ingredients thoroughly and sprinkle evenly over the batter in the pan.

SERVES 9

✳ Cardamom Spice Coffee Cake

1 pound butter, softened
2¼ cups light brown sugar, firmly packed
4 eggs
2 teaspoons vanilla extract
4 cups flour
2 teaspoons baking powder
2½ teaspoons baking soda
1½ teaspoons powdered cardamom
½ teaspoon salt
2 cups sour cream
1 tablespoon cinnamon
½ cup macadamia nut bits
Confectioners' sugar for decoration

Preheat the oven to 350 degrees. Grease and flour a 10-inch tube or bundt pan.

Cream together the butter and 2 cups of the sugar until light and fluffy. Add the eggs and vanilla and beat well. Sift together the flour, baking powder, baking soda, cardamom and salt in another mixing bowl. Add the dry ingredients to the creamed mixture alternately with the sour cream, beginning and ending with the flour mixture. Do not overmix.

Combine the remaining ¼ cup of brown sugar, cinnamon and macadamias in a separate bowl. Spoon a third of the batter into the prepared pan and sprinkle half the nut mixture evenly over the top. Cover with another third of the batter; sprinkle with the remaining nut mixture; top with the remaining third of the batter.

Bake in the preheated oven for 1½ hours, or until a cake tester inserted into the center comes out clean. Cool in the pan for 10 minutes, then turn out of the pan and complete the cooling on a wire rack.

Sift confectioners' sugar over the top before slicing.

SERVES 10-12

Spicy Applesauce Cake

8 tablespoons (1 stick) butter,
  softened
¾ cup light brown sugar, firmly
  packed
2 eggs
2 tablespoons strong coffee
3 cups flour
1 teaspoon salt
2 teaspoons baking soda
1½ teaspoons cinnamon
1 teaspoon ground cloves
½ teaspoon ground allspice
2 cups applesauce
Grated rind of 1 lemon
1½ cups currants
1 cup macadamia nut bits

8-ounce package cream cheese,
  softened
8 tablespoons (1 stick) butter,
  softened
1 cup confectioners' sugar
1 tablespoon vanilla extract
1 tablespoon milk

Preheat the oven to 350 degrees. Grease and flour a 9-inch bundt pan.

Cream the butter in a bowl until light and fluffy. Gradually beat in the sugar, then beat in the eggs, one at a time. Add the coffee and mix well. Set the batter aside.

Sift together the flour, salt, baking soda and spices. Add one-third of the dry ingredients to the batter and blend; stir in half the applesauce; then blend in the second third of the flour mixture, followed by the remainder of the applesauce. Add the lemon rind, currants and macadamias to the remaining portion of the flour mixture, stir, and blend into the batter.

Bake in the preheated oven for about 40 minutes, or until a cake tester inserted into the center comes out clean. Cool for 10 minutes in the pan, then turn out onto a wire rack. Frost with Vanilla Buttercream Icing (below).

Vanilla Buttercream Icing

Cream together the cream cheese and butter in a medium-sized mixing bowl. Gradually mix in the confectioners' sugar. Add the vanilla and milk and beat until creamy.

SERVES 10-12

Macadamia Orange Tea Cake

2 cups unsifted flour
2 teaspoons baking powder
Grated rind of 1 orange
½ teaspoon baking soda
¼ teaspoon salt
½ teaspoon nutmeg
½ teaspoon cinnamon
2 tablespoons light brown
  sugar, firmly packed
8 tablespoons (1 stick) butter
¾ cup granulated sugar
2 eggs
Juice of 1 orange, plus enough
  milk to total 1 cup
¾ cup macadamia nut bits
¾ cup golden raisins

Glaze
1 cup confectioners' sugar
1 tablespoon milk

Preheat the oven to 350 degrees. Grease and flour a 9½-by-5¼-by-2¾-inch loaf pan.

Stir together the flour, baking powder, orange rind, baking soda, salt, spices and brown sugar. Cream the butter and granulated sugar in the large bowl of an electric mixer until light and fluffy. Beat in the eggs, one at a time. Fold in the flour mixture alternately with the orange juice mixture. Stir in the macadamias and raisins. Spoon the batter into the prepared loaf pan.

Bake in the preheated oven for 1 hour, or until a cake tester inserted in the center comes out clean. Cool in the pan for 10 minutes, then turn out onto a wire rack. Either glaze while still hot or dust with confectioners' sugar when completely cooled.

To make the glaze, combine the sugar and milk and spread over the warm cake. Allow to cool before serving.

SERVES 8

✹ Citrus-Glazed Sour Cream Cake

2 cups flour
1 teaspoon baking powder
1 teaspoon baking soda
1 cup macadamia nut bits
16 tablespoons (2 sticks)
  butter, softened
1 cup granulated sugar
3 eggs, separated
¾ cup sour cream
Finely grated rind of 1 large
  orange
Finely grated rind of 2 lemons
⅛ teaspoon salt

Citrus Glaze
¾ cup granulated sugar
2 tablespoons orange juice
2 tablespoons lemon juice

Preheat the oven to 350 degrees and adjust the rack to the lower third of the oven. Butter a 9-inch springform pan and dust with fine, dry breadcrumbs.

Sift together the flour, baking powder and baking soda. Dredge the macadamias with 2 tablespoons of the flour mixture.

Cream the butter in a medium-sized bowl with an electric mixer, add the sugar and beat well. Beat in the egg yolks, one at a time. Beating at lowest speed, add the sifted flour mixture and sour cream alternately, beginning and ending with the dry ingredients. Stir in the macadamias and grated citrus rinds.

Whip the egg whites and salt in another bowl until stiff peaks form. Fold lightly into the batter and pour into the prepared pan.

Bake in the preheated oven for 1 hour, or until a cake tester inserted in the center comes out clean.

Just before the cake is ready, prepare the citrus glaze. Mix the sugar, orange juice and lemon juice in a small saucepan. Bring to a boil, stirring occasionally, and keep warm.

When the cake is done, place it in its pan on a wire rack and prick the top with a sharp knife. Gradually brush the hot glaze over the cake until it has all been absorbed. Allow the cake to cool completely in the pan before removing the sides and bottom of the springform.

SERVES 10-12

Tropic Bird

✱ German Chocolate Cake Macadamia

4 ounces German sweet
  chocolate, cut into small pieces
½ cup boiling water
2¼ cups sifted flour
1 teaspoon baking soda
½ teaspoon salt
1 cup butter
2 cups granulated sugar
4 eggs, separated
1 teaspoon vanilla extract
1 cup buttermilk

Preheat the oven to 350 degrees. Grease and flour 3 9-inch round cake pans.

Melt the chocolate in the boiling water. Cool. Sift the flour, baking soda and salt together in a small bowl. Cream the butter and sugar with an electric mixer, beating until light and fluffy. Beat in the egg yolks, one at a time, beating well after each addition. Fold in the vanilla and melted chocolate. Add the flour mixture alternately with the buttermilk, beating well after each addition. Whip the egg whites until stiff peaks form and fold into the batter. Pour the batter into the prepared pans.

Bake in the preheated oven for 30 minutes, or until the cake springs back to the touch. Do not overbake! Cool in the pans for 15 minutes, then remove and finish cooling on wire racks. Spread Coconut Macadamia Filling (below) between the layers and ice the top with the remainder.

Coconut Macadamia Filling

1½ cups evaporated milk
1 cup granulated sugar
5 egg yolks
12 tablespoons (1½ sticks)
  butter
1½ teaspoons vanilla extract
2 cups flaked coconut
1½ cups macadamia nut bits

Combine the milk, sugar, egg yolks, butter and vanilla in a saucepan. Cook over medium heat, stirring constantly, for about 12 minutes, until the mixture thickens. Remove from the heat and add the coconut and macadamias. Cool until the mixture reaches a spreading consistency. (Refrigerate it if necessary to speed up the process.)

SERVES 8-10

Father and Son

Cinnamon Nut Flan

Breadcrumbs, for dusting pan
8 tablespoons (1 stick) butter,
  softened
½ cup granulated sugar
4 eggs, separated
1 cup ground macadamia nuts
3 tablespoons cinnamon
3 tablespoons finely grated
  lemon rind
Confectioners' sugar, for
  decoration

Preheat the oven to 350 degrees. Grease a 10-inch round layer pan, line the bottom with wax paper, then grease the wax paper and sprinkle with fine breadcrumbs.

Cream the butter and sugar in a medium-sized mixing bowl until light and fluffy. Beat in the egg yolks, two at a time. Add the macadamias, cinnamon and lemon rind. Whip the egg whites until stiff peaks form. Fold into the egg-yolk mixture. Pour the batter into the prepared pan and smooth the surface.

Bake in the preheated oven for 40 minutes, then cool for 10 minutes in the pan before turning out on a rack. When the flan has completely cooled, place an attractive paper doily on the cake and sift confectioners' sugar over the top. Remove the doily with care so as not to spoil the pattern made by the sugar.

SERVES 8-10

✱ Macadamia Nut Torte

1 cup granulated sugar
6 eggs, separated
Grated rind and juice of
  1 lemon
1 teaspoon cinnamon
1 cup ground macadamia nuts
½ cup toasted white
  breadcrumbs
½ teaspoon almond extract
Whipped cream and
  macadamia nut bits, for
  decoration

Preheat the oven to 350 degrees. Have ready an ungreased 8-inch springform pan.

Sift the sugar into a small bowl. Beat the egg yolks in another bowl. Add the sugar gradually and beat until light and lemon-colored. Mix in the lemon, cinnamon, macadamias, bread-crumbs and almond extract. Whip the egg whites until stiff peaks form and fold lightly into the batter. Pour into the pan.

Bake in the preheated oven for 40 minutes. Cool completely in the pan before carefully removing the rim. Serve topped with whipped cream and macadamia nut bits.

SERVES 8

✳ Pineapple Blitz Torte

8 tablespoons (1 stick) butter,
  softened
1¼ cups granulated sugar
4 eggs, separated
⅔ cup flour
¼ teaspoon salt
1 teaspoon baking powder
¼ cup milk
1 teaspoon vanilla extract
¾ cup macadamia nut bits

Preheat the oven to 350 degrees. Grease 2 8-inch round layer cake pans, line them with wax paper and grease again.

Cream together the butter and ½ cup of the sugar in a medium-sized bowl. Add the yolks and beat well. Sift together the flour, salt and baking powder in another bowl. Beat into the creamed mixture alternately with the milk. Pour into the prepared pans and bake in the preheated oven for 15 minutes.

Meanwhile, whip the egg whites until foamy. Add the remaining ¾ cup of sugar, a tablespoon at a time, and beat until soft peaks form. Fold in the vanilla.

Remove the cakes from the oven and immediately spread them with the meringue mixture. Sprinkle with macadamias and return to the oven for 15 more minutes. Cool in the pans. When completely cooled, remove from the pans and place one layer, meringue side down, on a platter. Spread with Pineapple Filling (below) and place the remaining layer on top of the filling, meringue side up.

Pineapple Filling

1 cup heavy cream
1½ tablespoons confectioners'
  sugar
1 cup crushed pineapple, well
  drained
¼ teaspoon vanilla extract

Whip the cream until stiff and fold in the remaining ingredients.

SERVES 8

✱ Lemon Macadamia Torte

1¼ cups egg whites (whites from
  10 medium-size eggs)
2 cups confectioners' sugar
2 tablespoons cornstarch
¼ teaspoon vanilla extract
1⅔ cups macadamia nut bits,
  ground to a paste

Preheat the oven to 275 degrees. Grease and flour 2 10-inch round cake pans.

Whip the egg whites until foamy. Gradually add half the sugar, beating until soft peaks form. Sift together the remaining sugar and cornstarch. Gently fold the dry ingredients into the egg whites, add the vanilla and stir gently. Fold in the ground macadamias. Divide the batter in half and spread into the prepared cake pans.

Bake in the preheated oven for 1½ hours, or until pale gold. Cool the layers briefly in the pans, then turn them out, carefully, onto wire racks. Assemble with Lemon Filling (below).

Spread half of the filling onto one of the layers and place the second layer on top. Ice its top and sides with the remaining filling, leaving the bottom layer exposed. Chill for at least an hour before serving.

Lemon Filling

4 tablespoons cornstarch
¾ cup cold water
⅓ cup fresh lemon juice
1 tablespoon grated lemon rind
1 cup granulated sugar
2 egg yolks
1½ tablespoons butter

Dissolve the cornstarch in the cold water in a medium-sized, heavy saucepan. Stir in the lemon juice, lemon rind and sugar. Cook over medium-high heat for about 10 minutes, stirring constantly until thickened. Remove from the heat and beat in the egg yolks, one at a time. Return the mixture to low heat and cook for 3 minutes more. Remove from the heat and stir in the butter. Cool, stirring occasionally to prevent a skin forming.

SERVES 10

Pearl Hermes Reef

✳ Chocolate Lovers' Nut Torte

1¼ cups (5-ounce can) whole macadamia nuts
⅓ cup cornstarch
½ cup granulated sugar
8 ounces semisweet chocolate
2 tablespoons instant coffee granules
⅓ cup water
4 eggs, separated
12 tablespoons (1½ sticks) butter, softened
Pinch of salt

Preheat the oven to 350 degrees. Grease and flour a 9-inch round cake pan.

Grind the nuts in the blender until fine. Combine with the cornstarch and half the sugar in a small bowl.

Melt the chocolate, instant coffee granules and water in a small saucepan over low heat. Allow to cool slightly, then stir in the egg yolks, one at a time. Return to the heat and stir until the mixture has thickened slightly. Remove from the heat and beat in the softened butter, cut into pieces. Stir in the nut mixture. Whip the egg whites with the remaining ¼ cup of sugar until stiff peaks form, then fold into the chocolate-nut mixture. Spread in the prepared pan.

Bake in the preheated oven for 30 to 40 minutes. Cool in the pan for 30 minutes, then turn out onto a wire rack. When completely cooled, ice with Mocha Icing (below).

Mocha Icing

6 ounces sweet chocolate, broken into pieces
2 tablespoons instant coffee granules
⅓ cup water

Melt the chocolate, coffee granules and water together in a small saucepan over medium heat. Cool to spreading consistency.

SERVES 8-10

✳ ✳ Kiwi Coconut Cake

5 ripe kiwi fruit
¼ cup white wine
2 egg yolks
½ cup granulated sugar
1 envelope unflavored gelatin
4 tablespoons water
2 cups heavy cream
1 tablespoon confectioners'
  sugar
2 cups shredded coconut
10 whole macadamia nuts, for
  decoration

2 eggs, separated, plus 2 yolks
¼ cup granulated sugar
6 tablespoons flour
2 tablespoons cornstarch
3 tablespoons cocoa powder
1 cup ground macadamia nuts

Preheat the oven to 425 degrees. Grease and flour a 9-inch springform pan.

Beat the egg yolks and 2 tablespoons of the sugar in a bowl until thick and lemon-colored. Whip the egg whites in another bowl until stiff peaks form; fold in the remaining sugar. Fold lightly into the egg-yolk mixture. Sift together the flour, cornstarch and cocoa powder and fold into the mixture. Stir in the ground macadamias.

Bake in the preheated oven for 15 minutes. Remove the spring-form sides, cool on a rack and cut into two layers. Fill the cake with Kiwi Filling (below) and let it stand about an hour to allow the gelatin to set fully before icing and decorating with coconut and whole macadamias.

Kiwi Filling and Icing

Peel the skins from the kiwi fruit, taking care not to nick them. Dice 2 of the kiwis and refrigerate the others. Mix the diced kiwis with the wine, egg yolks and sugar in a double boiler over medium heat and stir the mixture constantly until thickened. Do not allow it to boil. Remove the pan from the heat and turn the mixture into a bowl.

Dissolve the gelatin in the water in a small saucepan over low heat and add to the kiwi-wine mixture. Allow to cool.

Whip 1 cup of the cream until stiff and fold lightly into the thickened kiwi mixture. Fill the cake and allow it to stand.

Just before serving, whip the remaining cup of cream with the confectioners' sugar until stiff and spread over the top and sides of the cake. Slice the 3 remaining kiwis thinly and use them to decorate the top of cake. Press the coconut onto the sides of the cake and decorate the top with the whole macadamias.

SERVES 10-12

Blueberry Nut Cake

2 cups flour
2 cups granulated sugar
2 teaspoons baking soda
1 teaspoon cinnamon
½ teaspoon nutmeg
½ teaspoon salt
4 cups fresh blueberries
½ cup macadamia nut bits
8 tablespoons (1 stick) butter,
  melted
2 eggs, lightly beaten
1 cup confectioners' sugar, for
  decoration

Preheat the oven to 325 degrees. Grease and flour a 13-by-9-inch pan.

Sift together the flour, sugar, baking soda, cinnamon, nutmeg and salt in a large bowl and mix well. Add the blueberries, macadamias, melted butter and lighly beaten eggs and mix well together. Turn into the prepared pan.

Bake in the preheated oven for 1 hour, or until a cake tester inserted in the center comes out clean. Cool in the pan. Sift with confectioners' sugar before serving.

SERVES 10-12

Pineapple Carrot Cake Macadamia

1½ cups vegetable oil
2 cups granulated sugar
4 eggs
2 cups flour
1 teaspoon cinnamon
2 teaspoons baking soda
1 teaspoon salt
3 cups grated carrots
1 cup macadamia nut bits
8-ounce can crushed pineapple,
  drained

8-ounce package cream cheese,
  softened
8-ounce can crushed pineapple,
  drained

Preheat the oven to 350 degrees. Grease a 10-inch tube pan.

Blend together the oil, sugar and eggs and beat well. Sift together the flour, cinnamon, baking soda and salt in a separate bowl and add to the egg mixture. Stir thoroughly. Fold in the grated carrots, macadamias and pineapple and pour the batter into the prepared pan.

Bake in the preheated oven for 1 hour, or until a cake tester inserted in the center comes out clean. Cool the cake in the pan. When cold, remove from the pan and frost with Pineapple Cream Cheese Icing (below).

Pineapple Cream Cheese Icing

Beat together the cream cheese and crushed pineapple, using an electric mixer, until light and fluffy.

SERVES 10-12

Tropical Upside Down Cake

3 tablespoons butter
½ cup light brown sugar, firmly
  packed
8-ounce can pineapple slices,
  drained and halved
½ cup macadamia nut bits
8 tablespoons (1 stick) butter,
  softened
¾ cup granulated sugar
2 eggs
1 teaspoon vanilla extract
1¼ cups flour
1 teaspoon baking soda
½ teaspoon baking powder
½ teaspoon salt
¾ cup buttermilk
1 cup rolled oats
½ cup mashed ripe banana

Preheat the oven to 350 degrees.

Melt the 3 tablespoons butter in a 9-inch-square pan. Scatter the brown sugar over the butter. Arrange the pineapple slices and macadamias on top of the sugar.

Beat together the softened butter and sugar until light and fluffy. Blend in the eggs and vanilla. Combine the flour, baking soda, baking powder and salt in a separate bowl. Add the flour mixture to the egg mixture alternately with the buttermilk, beginning and ending with the dry ingredients. Stir in the oats and banana. Spoon the batter over the topping in the pan.

Bake in the preheated oven for 45 to 50 minutes, or until a cake tester inserted in the center comes out clean. As soon as the cake is done, loosen the sides from the pan and immediately invert it onto a serving plate.

Serve warm or cold with ice cream, if desired.

SERVES 10-12

Carrot Cake

1¼ cups vegetable oil
2 cups granulated sugar
2⅛ cups flour
2 teaspoons cinnamon
2 teaspoons baking powder
1 teaspoon salt
4 eggs
4 cups grated carrots
1 cup raisins
1 cup macadamia nut bits
Whole macadamia nuts, for
  decoration

Preheat the oven to 350 degrees. Grease and flour a 10-inch springform pan.

Mix the oil and sugar together in a large mixing bowl. Sift together the flour, cinnamon, baking powder and salt in another bowl. Combine half of the flour mixture with the vegetable oil mixture. Add the eggs, one at a time, and mix well. Add the remaining flour mixture, then stir in the carrots, raisins and macadamia bits. Turn into the prepared pan.

Bake in the preheated oven for 70 minutes, or until a cake tester inserted into the center comes out clean. Remove the springform sides and cool on a rack. When completely cooled, frost with Vanilla Buttercream Icing (see page 22) and decorate with whole macadamias.

SERVES 10-12

Cardamom Wedding Torte

8 egg yolks, at room
  temperature
1 cup granulated sugar
2¼ cups macadamia nut bits
3 tablespoons flour
1½ teaspoons baking powder
½ teaspoon powdered cardamom
½ teaspoon cinnamon
½ teaspoon ginger
8 egg whites, at room
  temperature
¼ teaspoon cream of tartar

Preheat the oven to 350 degrees. Grease 4 8-inch round cake pans, line them with wax paper, and then grease again.

Beat the egg yolks until frothy in a large bowl with an electric mixer. Gradually add the sugar, beating constantly. Beat 4 to 5 more minutes at highest speed, or until the mixture is stiff.

Toss together the macadamias, flour, baking powder, cardamom, cinnamon and ginger. Beat the egg whites with the cream of tartar until soft peaks form. Fold the nut-flour mixture into the beaten egg whites with a few swift strokes of a spatula. Carefully fold the yolk-sugar mixture into the whites. Do not overfold—streaks of white should be visible in the batter. Spoon the batter into the prepared pans.

Bake in the preheated oven for 20 minutes, or until a cake tester inserted in the center of each cake comes out clean. Allow to cool in the pans for 10 minutes, then remove the pans and finish the cooling process on wire racks.

When the cakes have completely cooled, spread Orange Buttercream Frosting (below) between the layers and ice the top and sides.

Orange Buttercream Frosting

2 8-ounce packages cream
  cheese, softened
6 tablespoons butter, softened
2 egg yolks
2 cups granulated sugar
Grated rind of 3 oranges
2 tablespoons lemon juice

Beat the cream cheese and butter together until fluffy. Mix in the egg yolks, sugar, orange rind and lemon juice and beat until smooth.

If you prefer, you can beat 1 cup of heavy cream with ½ cup powdered sugar and 1 teaspoon vanilla extract and use instead of frosting on the top and sides of the cake.

MAKES 1 8-INCH ROUND 4 LAYER CAKE
SERVES 8-10

Note: This recipe doubles and quadruples easily, provided you use an electric mixer. Substitute sheet cake pans for the round ones.

Orange Nut Cake

3 eggs
6-ounce can frozen orange juice
  concentrate
1 cup sugar
2 cups graham cracker crumbs
1 teaspoon baking powder
½ teaspoon salt
1 cup macadamia nut bits
8-ounce package pitted dates,
  chopped
1 teaspoon vanilla extract
2 tablespoons sifted
  confectioners' sugar, optional

Preheat the oven to 350 degrees. Grease and flour a 9-inch-square pan.

Beat the eggs until light and fluffy. Beat in the orange juice. Add the sugar, graham cracker crumbs, baking powder, salt, macadamias, dates and vanilla and mix well. Pour the mixture into the prepared pan.

Bake in the preheated oven for 50 minutes, or until a cake tester inserted in the center comes out clean. Cool in the pan on a wire rack. When completely cooled, dust with confectioners' sugar or frost with Orange Icing (below).

Orange Icing

1¼ cups confectioners' sugar
3½ tablespoons orange juice

Combine the ingredients and beat until smooth and shiny.

SERVES 9-12

Morning Glory

Pies

The expression, "easy as pie," is certainly a misleading cliché, at least for the conscientious cook. A good pie is a labor of love. Too much flour toughens a crust; too much water makes it soggy. And too much shortening makes the dough greasy. We have come up with an easy no-fail crust; our basic pastry shell (page 40) tastes great and flutes perfectly.

Fillings for these pies vary from the usual fare. We have added nuts and sour cream to a deep-dish apple pie, nuts and strawberries to a juicy rhubarb pie, and used nuts as a decoration in several pies.

For your convenience the pies, with crusts, are listed in pairs. You may, of course, mix and match.

A Macadamia Plantation

Strawberry Cheese Pie

Filling
1 cup heavy cream
8-ounce package cream cheese,
* softened*
½ cup granulated sugar
1 teaspoon vanilla

Topping
2 cups strawberries, thinly
* sliced*
1 tablespoon cornstarch
1 tablespoon Triple Sec
1 cup macadamia nut bits

Prepare a 9-inch Pastry Shell (below) and bake it blind. Beat the cream in a small bowl until stiff. Beat the cream cheese, sugar and vanilla in another bowl and fold into the whipped cream. Pour into the crust and refrigerate for 1 hour.

Stir the cornstarch and triple sec in a medium-sized pan over low heat until thickened. Remove from the heat and cool. When completely cold, stir in the strawberries and spread the topping over the pie. Sprinkle macadamias on top.

SERVES 8

Pastry Shell

1 cup flour
½ teaspoon salt
3 tablespoons unsalted butter,
* frozen*
3 tablespoons shortening
2-3 tablespoons ice water

Mix together the flour and salt in a small bowl. Grate the frozen butter into the bowl and add the shortening. Cut in the butter and shortening, using a pastry blender or two knives, until they are evenly distributed and the mixture looks like coarse breadcrumbs. Add the water a tablespoon at a time, tossing with a fork until the pastry is moistened. Working quickly, form the dough into a ball with your fingers. Do not overwork! Wrap the ball in wax paper and chill it for at least 30 minutes.

Set the dough on a sheet of floured wax paper and roll out from center to edge until it is ⅛ inch thick, using flour as needed to prevent it sticking. Put the pastry into the pie plate and trim ½ to 1 inch beyond the edge; fold under and flute the rim.

SERVES 6-8

Lenore's Cheese Pie

2 8-ounce packages cream
  cheese, softened
1 cup sour cream
3 eggs, separated
1 cup sugar
3 tablespoons flour

Preheat the oven to 325 degrees. Prepare Graham Cracker Crumb-Nut Crust (below) in a 9-inch springform pan, bake and cool.

Beat the cream cheese and sour cream together until smooth. Beat in the egg yolks and sugar. Sift in the flour and stir to mix. Beat the egg whites until stiff peaks form and fold into the mixture. Pour into the prepared crust.

Bake in the preheated oven for 25 minutes, then turn off the oven. *Do not open the oven door!* Let the pie cool for 1 hour in the oven. Refrigerate all day or overnight before serving.

Graham Cracker Crumb-Nut Crust

1 cup graham cracker crumbs
½ cup macadamia nut bits
¼ cup granulated sugar
4 tablespoons (½ stick) butter,
  softened

Preheat the oven to 375 degrees.

Combine the graham cracker crumbs, macadamias and sugar in a large bowl. Blend in the softened butter. Press the mixture into a 9-inch springform pan or pie plate. Bake for 6 to 9 minutes. Cool.

SERVES 6-8

Orange Yogurt Cream Cheese Pie

12 ounces (1½ packages)
  cream cheese, softened
½ cup plain yogurt
¼ cup honey
½ teaspoon vanilla extract
1 tablespoon orange liqueur
Grated rind of 1 orange
¼ cup finely crushed graham
  cracker crumbs

Prepare a 9-inch Unbaked Graham Cracker Honey-Nut Crust (below) and refrigerate until the filling is ready.

Beat the cream cheese in a medium-sized bowl until fluffy. Beat in all the remaining ingredients (except the graham cracker crumbs) one after the other until the mixture is smooth. Spread carefully into the prepared shell and top with the cracker crumbs. Chill for at least 3 hours before serving.

Unbaked Graham Cracker Honey-Nut Crust

¾ cup finely crushed graham
  cracker crumbs
½ cup macadamia nut bits
8 tablespoons (½ stick) butter,
  melted
2 tablespoons honey
1 teaspoon cinnamon
Dash of nutmeg

Combine all the ingredients thoroughly in a small bowl. Press firmly onto the sides and bottom of a 9-inch pie plate and refrigerate.

SERVES 6-8

✳ Macadamia Lemon-Rum Chiffon Pie

1 tablespoon gelatin
¼ cup cold water
4 eggs, separated
1 cup granulated sugar
½ teaspoon salt
½ cup hot water
Grated rind of 1 lemon
2 tablespoons rum or
  1 teaspoon vanilla extract
1 cup macadamia nut bits,
  toasted
Whipped cream, for decoration

Prepare a 9-inch Butter Crust (below), bake blind and allow to cool.

Soften the gelatin in the cold water and set aside. Beat the egg yolks in a medium-sized saucepan and add ½ cup of the sugar, salt, hot water and lemon rind. Cook over medium heat for about 5 minutes until thickened, stirring constantly. Stir the gelatin into the hot mixture. Remove from the heat and cool to room temperature. Stir in the rum, or vanilla, and ¾ cup of the macadamias. Mix well.

Beat the egg whites until soft peaks form. Gradually add the remaining ½ cup sugar and fold the whites gently into the yolk mixture. Pour into the cooled pie crust and chill for at least 4 hours.

Just before serving, spread with a thin layer of whipped cream and sprinkle with the remaining ¼ cup of macadamias.

Butter Crust

8 tablespoons (1 stick) butter,
  softened
 2 tablespoons granulated sugar
1 cup flour

Preheat the oven to 375 degrees. Have ready a 9-inch pie pan.

Beat the butter and sugar together. Mix in the flour just until a dough forms. (If using an electric mixer, mix at lowest speed.) Flour your fingers thoroughly and press the mixture evenly into the pie pan. Flute the edges.

Bake in the preheated oven for 12 to 15 minutes, or until golden-brown. Cool.

SERVES 8

Macadamia Coconut Pie

8 tablespoons (1 stick) butter,
 softened
¾ cup granulated sugar
3 eggs
¾ cup dark corn syrup
½ cup shredded coconut
¼ teaspoon salt
1 teaspoon vanilla extract
1 cup macadamia nut bits

Preheat the oven to 350 degrees. Prepare an 8-inch Pastry Shell (see page 40), but do not bake.

Cream the butter, using the electric mixer, until fluffy. Add sugar gradually and continue to beat until lemon-colored. Add the eggs, one after the other, beating after each addition. Blend in the corn syrup. Add coconut, salt, vanilla and corn syrup and mix well. Pour the filling in the unbaked pie shell.

Bake in the preheated oven for 35-40 minutes. Cool completely in the pan before serving.

SERVES 6

✱ Sour Cream Apple Pie
('Awa Kalima Apala Pai)

5 large tart apples
1 tablespoon lemon juice
¾ cup granulated sugar
2 tablespoons flour
1 teaspoon cinnamon
¼ teaspoon freshly ground
 nutmeg
¼ teaspoon salt
¾ cup macadamia nut bits
4 tablespoons (½ stick) butter,
 softened
1 cup sour cream

Preheat the oven to 350 degrees. Prepare Pastry Shell (see page 40) but do not bake.

Wash, peel and core the apples. Cut them into thin, uniform slices and arrange in overlapping rows in the bottom of the pastry shell. Sprinkle with lemon juice.

Blend together the sugar, flour, cinnamon, nutmeg and salt. Stir in the macadamias. Cut in the butter, using a pastry blender or your fingers, until the mixture resembles breadcrumbs. Stir in the sour cream and spread evenly over the apples.

Bake in the preheated oven for 50 minutes or until the apples are tender. Serve hot or cold.

SERVES 6-8

The Hamakua Coast

Hawaiian Apple Pie

12-ounce can (1½ cups)
  unsweetened pineapple juice
¾ cup granulated sugar
7 cooking apples, peeled, cored
  and cut into thin wedges
3 tablespoons cornstarch
1 tablespoon butter
½ teaspoon cinnamon
¼ teaspoon nutmeg
½ teaspoon salt
½ teaspoon vanilla extract
1 cup heavy cream
1 cup macadamia nut bits,
  finely chopped and lightly
  toasted

Prepare a 9-inch Macadamia Pie Crust (below), bake and allow to cool.

Combine 1¼ cups of the pineapple juice and the sugar in a large saucepan and bring to a boil. Add the apples and simmer, covered, for 3 to 4 minutes, or until the apples are tender but not soft. Lift the apples from the liquid with a slotted spoon and set them aside to drain. Slowly blend the remaining pineapple juice into the cornstarch and stir this into the hot liquid in the saucepan. Cook and stir until thickened and bubbly. Cook 1 minute more. Remove from the heat, stir in the butter, cinnamon, nutmeg, salt and vanilla. Let stand 30 minutes, without stirring.

Pour half the filling into the prepared shell. Spread to cover the bottom of the pastry. Arrange the reserved apples on top and spoon the remaining filling over all.

Cover and chill. When you are ready to serve, whip the cream. Spread it over the pie and sprinkle with the chopped macadamias.

SERVES 8

Macadamia Pie Crust

1¼ cup flour
Pinch of salt
½ cup macadamia nuts, finely
  chopped
7 tablespoons vegetable
  shortening
2 tablespoons ice water

Preheat the oven to 425 degrees. Have ready a 9-inch pie plate.

Combine the flour, salt and macadamias in a large bowl. Cut in the shortening with a pastry blender or two knives until the mixture resembles fine breadcrumbs. Sprinkle ice water on the mixture and mold the dough gently into a ball, using your fingers. (Chill for 20 minutes before rolling).

Put the dough on a sheet of floured wax paper and roll out from center to edge until about ⅛ inch thick. Press into the pie plate.

Bake in the preheated oven at 425 degrees for 5 to 10 minutes, until golden, then reduce the heat to 350 degrees and bake for another 8 minutes. Cool before filling.

SERVES 8

✳ Strawberry Rhubarb Pie
(Ohelo-Papa Rhubarb Pai)

4 cups fresh (or frozen without
  sugar) rhubarb, cut diagonally
  into 1-inch slices
1 pint (2 cups) fresh
  strawberries, sliced
¼ cup flour
1 teaspoon lemon juice
1¼ cups granulated sugar

Topping
3 tablespoons flour
2 tablespoons granulated sugar
1 teaspoon freshly ground
  nutmeg
¾ cup macadamia nut bits
2 tablespoons butter

Preheat the oven to 450 degrees. Prepare a 9-inch Pastry Shell, following recipe on page 40. Before baking, brush the shell with 1 lightly beaten egg white. Bake in the preheated oven for 10 to 12 minutes, or until lightly colored. Set the pastry aside to cool and reduce oven temperature to 350 degrees.

Combine the rhubarb, strawberries, flour, lemon juice and sugar in a large bowl. Let the mixture stand at room temperature for 15 minutes, then spoon it into the cooled pastry shell.

To make the topping, blend together the 3 tablespoons flour, 2 tablespoons sugar, nutmeg and macadamias. Sprinkle evenly over the pie filling and dot with butter.

Bake the pie at 350 degrees for 45 to 50 minutes, or until the filling has completely set. Serve cold.

SERVES 6-8

Banana Pukini Pai

⅓ cup granulated sugar
1 tablespoon flour
⅛ teaspoon salt
2 egg yolks, lightly beaten
1 cup whole milk, scalded
1 tablespoon lemon juice
½ cup heavy cream
2 medium-size bananas, thinly
  sliced
½ cup whole macadamia nuts
Finely chopped macadamia nut
  bits, for decoration

Prepare a 9-inch Butter Crust (see page 43), bake and allow to cool completely.

Combine the sugar, flour and salt in the top of a double boiler over boiling water. Stir in the egg yolks, then gradually stir in the scalded milk, making sure all the ingredients are well blended. Cook for about 15 minutes, stirring constantly, until the mixture resembles a thick pudding. Remove from the heat, cool and then chill, stirring occasionally to prevent a skin forming. When thoroughly chilled, add the lemon juice and half the cream.

Line the baked shell with bananas and whole nuts. Cover with the creamy mixture. Chill. Just before serving, whip the remaining cream and spread over the top. Sprinkle chopped nuts over all.

SERVES 6-8

Blueberry Cream Pie

1 cup heavy cream
¼ cup confectioners' sugar
½ teaspoon vanilla extract
1 cup fresh blueberries
½ teaspoon cinnamon
¼ teaspoon freshly ground
  nutmeg

Prepare a 9-inch Macadamia Nut Crust (see below), bake and allow to cool.

Whip the cream with the sugar and vanilla. Fold in the blueberries and spices. Pile into the prepared crust.

Note: Substitute any berries in season.

Macadamia Nut Crust

3 tablespoons butter, melted
3 tablespoons granulated sugar
2 cups macadamia nut bits

Preheat the oven to 350 degrees. Have ready a 9-inch pie plate.

Combine the butter, sugar and macadamias in a small bowl and mix well. Press the crumb mixture onto the bottom and sides of the pie plate to form an even crust.

Bake in the preheated oven for 10 minutes. Cool before filling.

SERVES 8

Meg's Macadamia Nut Pie

3 eggs
2 tablespoons butter, melted
2 tablespoons flour
¼ teaspoon vanilla extract
⅛ teaspoon salt
½ cup granulated sugar
1½ cups dark corn syrup
1½ cups whole macadamia nuts

Preheat the oven to 425 degrees. Prepare an 8-inch Pastry Shell (see page 40), but do not bake.

Beat the eggs in a medium-sized bowl and stir in the melted butter, flour, vanilla, salt, sugar and syrup. Spread the macadamias on the bottom of the unbaked pastry shell and gently spoon the filling over them.

Bake in the preheated oven for 10 minutes at 425 degrees, then reduce the heat to 325 degrees and bake for 40 minutes more, or until the custard is set.

SERVES 6-8

✳ Macadamia Pineapple Cream Pie

¾ cup granulated sugar
⅓ cup cornstarch
⅛ teaspoon salt
3 cups milk
4 egg yolks, beaten
2 tablespoons butter
20-ounce can unsweetened
  crushed pineapple, drained
⅓ cup macadamia nut bits
1 cup heavy cream
2 tablespoons dark rum

Prepare a 9-inch Graham Cracker Crumb-Nut Crust (see page 41), bake and allow to cool.

Combine the sugar, cornstarch and salt in a heavy saucepan. Gradually stir in the milk and egg yolks. Bring the mixture to a boil, stirring constantly, and boil and stir for about 1 minute, or until the mixture thickens. Remove from the heat and stir in the butter until it is incorporated in the hot custard. Pour the custard into a bowl, cover with wax paper or plastic wrap to prevent a skin forming, cool and chill for about 1 hour.

Stir the pineapple and nuts into the cooled custard. Whip ½ cup of the cream with the rum in a small bowl until stiff, and fold into the custard. Spoon the mixture into the prepared pie shell and chill.

Just before serving, whip the remaining cream and spoon over the top of the pie.

SERVES 6-8

Bird of Paradise

Cookies and Bars

No cookbook on baking would be complete without a section on cookies. We've chosen a tasty and diverse sampling, ranging in shape from ball to bar and in flavor from chocolate to lemon, all enhanced by macadamia nuts. Whether you want cookies for the children's after-school snack, an elegant afternoon tea, or a special holiday get-together, you'll find them here. Most of them freeze well, so you can prepare them days in advance, or just keep a ready supply on hand.

The chapter begins with some traditional macaroons. These dainty cookies (delicious with tea!) are easy to prepare, but because they can take quite a while to bake, they should be started well ahead of time. Crisp Macadamia Lace, rich Basque Nut and sugar-dusted Snowball cookies could be combined to make up a lovely assorted tray for a special occasion. We've included a selection of bar cookies, most of them very simple to make, with flavors to tempt everyone: chocolate, coconut, cinnamon, date, lemon, rum and apricot. These versatile cookies lend themselves equally well to plain or fancy occasions.

We conclude with that all-time favorite, the brownie. Margot's Brownies, rich and chewy, are a treat for the true chocolate lover. A luscious and pretty variation is marbled with cream cheese. Butterscotch and chocolate are melded in delectable brownies affectionately known as "Blondies." Finally, a recipe developed especially for us by Mauna Loa offers a cakier, less chocolaty brownie that emphasizes the macadamia nut's flavor.

A young "Wahine"

Macadamia Nut Meringue Cookies

4 egg whites
1 cup granulated sugar
3 cups ground macadamia nut
  bits

Preheat the oven to 275 degrees. Lightly grease a cookie sheet.

Put the egg whites and sugar in the top of a double boiler and bring the water in the bottom to a full boil. When the water begins to boil, start beating the egg white mixture and continue until stiff peaks form (this is easiest with a hand-held electric mixer or whisk).

Remove from the heat and fold in the ground macadamias. Drop by spoonfuls onto the cookie sheet about 1 inch apart. Bake in the preheated oven for about 12 minutes, or until lightly browned and crisp. Remove from the sheet immediately and cool on a wire rack.

MAKES 3 DOZEN

Macadamia Macaroons

3 egg whites, divided
2 cups macadamia nut bits,
  ground into a paste
1 cup granulated sugar
Whole macadamia nuts, for
  decoration

Preheat the oven to 325 degrees. Butter and flour 2 cookie sheets.

Beat 1 egg white in a small bowl until stiff peaks form. Fold in the macadamia paste. Beat the remaining egg whites in another bowl until stiff, and beat in the sugar. Fold the 2 mixtures together until smooth.

Drop the mixture by teaspoonfuls onto the cookie sheets about 1 inch apart. Put a whole macadamia nut in the center of each cookie. Bake in the preheated oven for 15 minutes, or until lightly colored. Remove from sheets at once and cool on wire racks.

MAKES 4 DOZEN

Macadamia Walnut Meringues

2 egg whites, at room
  temperature
¼ teaspoon cream of tartar
⅛ teaspoon salt
½ teaspoon vanilla extract
½ cup granulated sugar
½ cup macadamia nut bits,
  finely chopped
½ cup walnuts, finely chopped

Preheat the oven to 250 degrees. Line 2 cookie sheets with foil and grease them lightly.

Beat the egg whites, cream of tartar and salt in a large bowl until foamy. Add the vanilla and continue beating adding sugar 1 tablespoon at a time until stiff peaks form (this will take about 3 minutes). Fold in the macadamias.

Drop by rounded teaspoonfuls, 1 inch apart, onto the prepared sheets.

Bake in the preheated oven for 1 hour, then turn off the heat and leave the meringues in the oven for 1 hour more. *Do not open the door!* Take from sheets, cool completely. Store the meringues in airtight containers.

MAKES ABOUT 2 DOZEN

Note: To make shells to hold ice cream or fruit, spoon the meringue batter into a pastry bag and squeeze out onto the cookie sheet in a spiral pattern, to form small bowls. Bake as directed above, and fill as desired.

Coconut Macaroons

2 egg whites, at room
  temperature
2 teaspoons coffee liqueur
½ teaspoon vanilla extract
¼ teaspoon salt
⅔ cup granulated sugar
¾ cup flaked coconut
¼ cup macadamia nut bits

Preheat the oven to 250 degrees. Grease 2 baking sheets.

Beat the egg whites, liqueur, vanilla and salt in a large bowl with an electric mixer until soft peaks form. Gradually add the sugar, 1 tablespoon at a time, and continue to beat until stiff peaks form. Fold in the coconut.

Drop by teaspoonfuls, 2 inches apart, onto the prepared cookie sheets. Sprinkle the cookies with macadamias.

Bake in the preheated oven for about 1 hour, until browned and crisp. Remove from the sheets at once. Cool on wire racks.

MAKES ABOUT 2 DOZEN

Macadamia Lace Cookies

8 tablespoons (1 stick) butter
½ cup light corn syrup
½ cup light brown sugar, firmly
 packed
4 teaspoons unsweetened cocoa
 powder
½ teaspoon cinnamon
1 cup flour
½ cup macadamia nut bits

Preheat the oven to 375 degrees. Lightly grease 2 cookie sheets.

Bring the butter, corn syrup and brown sugar to a boil in a medium-sized saucepan, stirring constantly. Combine the cocoa, cinnamon, flour and macadamias in a small bowl, and gradually stir into the hot butter mixture. Drop by level tablespoons, about 3 inches apart, onto the prepared cookie sheets.

Bake in the preheated oven for 5 to 6 minutes, until golden brown and bubbling. Cool on the sheets for a minute or two and then turn onto a wire cooling rack.

MAKES 2 DOZEN

Macadamia Cream Cookies

2 ounces unsweetened chocolate,
 cut into small pieces
12 tablespoons (1½ sticks)
 butter, softened
1⅓ cups granulated sugar
1 teaspoon vanilla extract
1 egg
½ cup sour cream
¾ cups flour
½ teaspoon baking soda
½ teaspoon baking powder
½ teaspoon salt
½ cup macadamia nut bits

Preheat the oven to 425 degrees. Grease 2 cookie sheets.

Melt the chocolate in a double boiler over boiling water. Cream the butter in the large bowl of an electric mixer, and gradually beat in the sugar. Add the vanilla and egg, and continue beating until fluffy. Stir in the melted chocolate and then the sour cream, blending well. Sift together the flour, baking soda, baking powder and salt in a separate bowl, then add to the batter and mix well. Stir in the macadamias. Drop by teaspoonfuls onto the prepared cookie sheets about 1 inch apart.

Bake in the preheated oven for 8-10 minutes. Remove from the sheets at once and cool on wire racks.

MAKES 4 DOZEN

Basque Nut Cookies

2 cups unsifted flour
16 tablespoons (2 sticks) butter, softened
½ cup light brown sugar, firmly packed
Grated rind of 1 orange
1 cup macadamia nut bits

Preheat the oven to 325 degrees. Have ready, but do not grease, a cookie sheet.

Stir together the flour, butter, brown sugar and orange rind in a medium-sized bowl until the mixture forms a small ball. Stir in the macadamias. Wrap in wax paper and chill for about 30 minutes. Form into ½-inch balls, place on the cookie sheet, 1 inch apart and press with a fork to flatten.

Bake in the preheated oven for 20 minutes, or until golden brown. Remove from the sheet at once and cool on a wire rack.

MAKES 2½ DOZEN

Snowballs

16 tablespoons (2 sticks) butter, softened
1 cup confectioners' sugar
2¼ cups flour
¼ teaspoon baking soda
1 teaspoon vanilla extract
1 cup finely chopped macadamia nut bits

Preheat the oven to 400 degrees. Have ready, but do not grease 2 cookie sheets.

Cream together the butter and ½ cup of the sugar. Sift the flour and baking soda into the butter mixture and stir in. Add the vanilla and half the macadamias and mix well. Form into 1-inch balls and place on the prepared cookie sheets, 1 inch apart.

Bake in the preheated oven for 15 minutes, until lightly colored. Remove from the oven and allow to cool slightly on the sheets. Combine the remaining ½ cup of sugar and the rest of the macadamias in a small bowl. While the balls are still hot, roll them in the sugar-nut mixture and set on wire racks to cool completely.

MAKES 4 DOZEN

✴ Chocolate-Topped Macadamia Nut Cookies

18 tablespoons (2¼ sticks)
  butter, softened
1 cup confectioners' sugar
2 eggs
3 tablespoons milk
Grated rind of 1 lemon
4½ cups flour, sifted
1¾ cups macadamia nut bits

Cream the butter and sugar in the large bowl of an electric mixer until light and fluffy. Beat in the eggs, one at a time. Stir in the milk and lemon rind. Gradually work the flour and macadamias into the creamed mixture to form a dough.

Roll out half the dough into a long thin rope about 1 inch in diameter. Flatten the dough to form a strip about 1½ inches wide. Repeat with the remaining dough. Wrap the strips in wax paper and chill for at least 2 hours.

When ready to bake the cookies, preheat the oven to 400 degrees and grease 2 cookie sheets.

Cut the chilled strips of dough into pieces 1 inch long and place on the prepared sheets. Bake in the preheated oven for 15 minutes, or until golden brown. Cool on wire racks. When completely cooled, spread with Chocolate Topping (below) and return to the wire cooling rack until the chocolate has completely set.

Chocolate Topping

4 ounces semisweet chocolate,
  cut into small pieces
1¾ cups macadamia nut bits

Melt the chocolate over low heat in a double boiler. Spread the warm chocolate thickly over the cookies, sprinkle with macadamias and allow to set.

MAKES 2 DOZEN

Waihoi Valley

✱ Frozen Chocolate Macadamia Nut Squares

8 tablespoons (1 stick) butter,
  melted
1½ cups confectioners' sugar
3 eggs, lighlty beaten
3 ounces semisweet chocolate,
  melted
2 cups crushed vanilla wafers
1 cup heavy whipping cream
1 tablespoon granulated sugar
2 teaspoons vanilla extract
1½ cups macadamia nut bits

Grease a 9-inch-square pan.

Cream the melted butter with the confectioners' sugar in a medium-sized bowl. Add the eggs and the melted chocolate and continue beating until light and fluffy.

Press the crushed vanilla wafers into the prepared pan. Gently spoon the chocolate mixture over the vanilla wafers, making sure it extends to the corners of the pan.

Whip the cream with the tablespoon granulated sugar and vanilla until stiff, then spread it evenly over the chocolate mixture in the pan. Sprinkle the macadamias over the top.

Freeze for 2-3 hours until firm and cut into 1½-inch squares.

MAKES 3 DOZEN

Coconut Chews

2 eggs
2 cups firmly packed light
  brown sugar
⅛ teaspoon salt
½ teaspoon vanilla extract
2 cups shredded coconut
½ cup macadamia nut bits,
  toasted
6 tablespoons flour

Preheat the oven to 350 degrees. Grease and flour a 9-inch-square cake pan.

Beat the eggs in a large bowl until foamy. Beat in the brown sugar, salt and vanilla. Add the coconut and macadamias. Fold in the flour. Spread into the prepared pan.

Bake in the preheated oven for 30 minutes, or until golden brown. Let cool 10 to 15 minutes before cutting into 1½-inch squares. Let cool completely before removing the cookies from the pan.

MAKES 3 DOZEN

Cinnamon Squares

2 cups sifted flour
1½ tablespoons cinnamon
1 teaspoon salt
8 tablespoons (1 stick) butter
8 tablespoons (1 stick)
  margarine
1 cup granulated sugar
1 egg, separated
1½ cups macadamia nut bits

Preheat the oven to 325 degrees. Grease and flour a 15 ½-by-10 ½-by-1-inch pan.

Sift together the flour, cinnamon and salt. Cream the butter, margarine and sugar in the large bowl of an electric mixer. Beat in the egg yolk and the sifted dry ingredients. Press the dough into the prepared pan.

Beat the egg white until foamy and paint a thin layer on the batter. Press the macadamias on top of this, to cover the full extent of the pan.

Bake in the preheated oven for 30 minutes, until lightly colored. Cut into 2-inch squares. Cool in the pan.

MAKES 2 DOZEN

Macadamia Nut-Rum Bars

Cookie Crust
8 tablespoons (1 stick) butter,
  softened
¼ cup granulated sugar
1 cup flour

Filling
2 eggs, lightly beaten
1¼ cups light brown sugar,
  firmly packed
2 tablespoons flour
½ teaspoon salt
¼ teaspoon baking powder
1 cup flaked coconut
1 cup macadamia nut bits
1 teaspoon vanilla extract
1 tablespoon rum

Preheat the oven to 350 degrees. Have ready a 9-by-13-inch or 8-by-10-inch cake pan.

Make the crust by mixing the butter, sugar and flour together in a small bowl until thoroughly blended. Press the mixture evenly over the bottom of the cake pan.

Bake in the preheated oven for 15 to 20 minutes, until just beginning to brown.

Meanwhile, make the filling by stirring all the ingredients together in a mixing bowl until well blended. Spread over the baked crust. Return to the oven and bake 15 to 20 minutes longer, until the filling is firm and golden brown.

MAKES 2 DOZEN

❋ Lemon-Coconut-Nut Squares

1¼ cups light brown sugar,
   firmly packed
8 tablespoons (1 stick) butter,
   softened
1½ cups flour
2 eggs, lightly beaten
1½ cups shredded coconut
1 cup macadamia nut bits
2 tablespoons flour
½ teaspoon baking powder
¼ teaspoon salt
½ teaspoon vanilla extract

1 cup confectioners' sugar
1 tablespoon butter, melted
Grated rind and juice of
   1 lemon

Preheat the oven to 275 degrees. Grease a 13-by-9-by-2-inch pan.

Cream together ½ cup of the brown sugar and the butter. Stir in the flour. Pat firmly into the prepared pan and bake for 10 minutes. Remove from the oven and increase the oven temperature to 350 degrees.

Combine the eggs, remaining brown sugar, coconut, macadamias, 2 tablespoons flour, baking powder, salt and vanilla in a large bowl. Spread on top of the baked mixture.

Bake for another 20 minutes, or until golden brown. While still warm, drizzle with Lemon Frosting (below). Allow to cool slightly before cutting into 2-inch squares. Let cool completely before removing the cookies from pan.

Lemon Frosting

Beat together all the ingredients in a small bowl. Drizzle the frosting onto the warm cookies.

MAKES 2 DOZEN

✱ Fruit-Filled Bars

Filling
⅓ cup each dried pitted dates,
  apricots and golden raisins,
  finely chopped
⅓ cup granulated sugar
¼ cup orange juice
⅓ cup water

Cookie Crust
1 cup flour
¼ teaspoon baking soda
½ teaspoon salt
½ cup light brown sugar, firmly
  packed
½ cup shortening
Grated rind of 1 orange
2 tablespoons milk
1½ cups rolled oats
¾ cup macadamia nut bits

Preheat the oven to 350 degrees. Generously grease a 9-inch-square pan.

To make the filling, combine the fruits, granulated sugar, orange juice and water in a saucepan. Cook for about 5 minutes, until thickened, then remove from the heat to cool.

To make the crust, sift together the flour, baking soda and salt in a medium-sized mixing bowl. Add the brown sugar, shortening, orange rind and milk, and blend until smooth. Stir in the oats and nuts and make into a ball of dough. Divide the dough in half and roll out each in turn between sheets of wax paper. Spread one half in the bottom of the prepared pan. Cover with the fruit mixture. Place the remaining sheet of dough over the filling and trim to fit the pan.

Bake in the preheated oven for 25 to 30 minutes, until golden brown. Partially cool before cutting into squares.

MAKES 2 DOZEN

Margot's Brownies

16 tablespoons (2 sticks) butter,
  softened
4 ounces baking chocolate, cut
  into small pieces
4 eggs
1 cup flour
2 cups granulated sugar
1 teaspoon vanilla extract
1 cup whole macadamia nuts

Preheat the oven to 325 degrees. Grease a 9-by-13-inch pan.

Melt the butter and chocolate slowly in a heavy saucepan over low heat. Remove from the heat and beat in the eggs, one at a time. Add the flour and sugar and beat until shiny. Stir in the vanilla and macadamias. Turn into the prepared pan.

Bake in the preheated oven for 45 minutes, or until a cake tester inserted in the center comes out clean. Cut into squares while still hot.

MAKES 2 DOZEN

Cream Cheese Swirl Brownies

16 tablespoons (2 sticks) butter, softened
4 ounces baking chocolate, cut into small pieces
2 cups granulated sugar
4 eggs
1 cup flour
1 teaspoon vanilla extract
½ teaspoon cinnamon
½ teaspoon salt
1 cup macadamia nut bits
8-ounce package cream cheese, softened

Preheat the oven to 350 degrees. Grease a 9-by-13-inch pan.

Melt the butter and chocolate in a heavy saucepan over low heat. Remove from the heat and blend in the sugar. Let cool, then add the eggs and beat well. Beat in the flour. Add the vanilla, cinnamon and salt and mix well. Stir in the macadamias and softened cream cheese. Turn into the prepared pan.

Bake in the preheated oven for 25 minutes, or until a cake tester inserted into the center comes out clean.

MAKES 2 DOZEN

Carole's Blondies

2⅔ cups flour, sifted
2½ teaspoons baking powder
½ teaspoon salt
6 tablespoons butter
2¼ cups firmly packed light brown sugar
3 eggs
1 cup macadamia nut bits
1 cup semisweet chocolate morsels

Preheat the oven to 350 degrees. Grease a 15-by-10-by-1-inch pan.

Sift together the flour, baking powder, and salt in a small bowl. Melt the butter in a large saucepan. Remove from the heat and stir in the brown sugar. Let cool for 10 minutes. Beat in the eggs, one at a time. Add the flour mixture and beat well. Stir in the macadamias and chocolate morsels. Spread in the prepared pan.

Bake in the preheated oven for 30 minutes, or until lightly colored.

MAKES 2 DOZEN

Mauna Loa Brownies

4 ounces baking chocolate, cut
  into small pieces
8 tablespoons (1 stick) butter
4 eggs
¼ teaspoon salt
1½ cups granulated sugar
6 tablespoons honey
½ teaspoon vanilla extract
1 cup flour
1 1/6 teaspoon baking soda
½ cup macadamia nut bits

Preheat the oven to 350 degrees. Grease a 13-by-9-inch cake pan.

Melt the chocolate and butter together in a small, heavy saucepan over medium heat; allow to cool slightly. Beat the eggs in a mixing bowl until light-colored and foamy. Beat in the salt. Gradually add the sugar, honey and vanilla, beating well after each addition. Fold the cooled chocolate mixture into the eggs and sugar, then gently stir in the flour, baking soda and macadamias. Turn into the prepared pan.

Bake in the preheated oven for 45 minutes, or until a cake tester inserted in the center comes out clean. (Don't be alarmed if the brownies look toffee-colored; the chocolate is lurking just beneath the crust.) Let cool in the pan before cutting into squares.

MAKES 2 DOZEN

A Booby Bird

Desserts

Collected here under the title of "Desserts" is a wonderfully diverse group of recipes, with something delectable for any occasion, whether it be brunch, tea, a casual supper or an elegant dinner party.

If you're looking for a simple and refreshing way to end (or begin) a meal, try one of our three fresh fruit compotes. Fruit salad takes on a tropical twist! Or, if you're in the mood for something a little richer, we offer several scrumptiously nutty desserts: nut-filled crepes smothered in mocha sauce, strudel with a ricotta-nut filling, or rolled macadamia baklava. These take a little more time to prepare, but are well worth it.

For chocolate lovers, this section has two options: a luscious chocolate mousse that takes only minutes to prepare and a chocolate mousse pie that takes several hours and is worthy of your most special guests. Both can be made well ahead of time.

We conclude with four variations of that always-elegant finale, the dessert soufflé. Macadamia nuts provide a delicious contrast to flavors ranging from a light and tangy lemon to an unusually delicate prune. Don't be scared by this classically temperamental and failure-prone dessert: all that is required for success is careful attention to measurements, oven temperature and baking time.

Looking toward Kaneohe and Kailua on Oahu

Hawaiian Fruit Cup

¾ cup water
3 tablespoons granulated sugar
½ teaspoon ground ginger
½ lemon
¼ cup orange liqueur
2 cups papaya or melon chunks
1 cup seeded red or green
 grapes
1 banana, cut into ½-inch slices
½ cup macadamia nut bits

Combine the water, sugar and ginger in a small saucepan and bring to a boil. Reduce the heat and simmer, covered, for 10 minutes. Cut the lemon into thin slices and cut each slice into 4 pieces. Remove the syrup from the heat, add the lemon pieces and cool to room temperature. Stir in the liqueur.

Combine the fruit and macadamias in a bowl. Pour the syrup over them and stir gently. Chill before serving.

SERVES 6

Tropical Compote

¼ cup macadamia nuts, halved
2 cups fresh pineapple, cut in
 ½-inch cubes
1 cup sweet apple cubes
 (skinned)
1 cup papaya cubes
1 cup guava cubes
1 cup ½-inch thick banana
 slices
1 cup medium-size whole
 strawberries
1 cup raspberries
1 orange, sliced, then halved
½ cup Cognac
½ cup Triple Sec
2 tablespoons granulated sugar

Gently combine the macadamias and fruit in a large bowl. Combine the liqueurs and pour over the nuts and fruit. Cover, and chill for a couple of hours. Sprinkle with the sugar and spoon into individual grapefruit or pineapple shells. Set in cracked ice and decorate with mint leaves.

SERVES 10-15

Tropical Fruits
Mauna Loa

¼ cup water
2 tablespoons granulated sugar
1 cinnamon stick
½ cup dark rum
2 cups pineapple chunks
1 cup papaya chunks
1 cup strawberry halves
1 cup mango chunks
1 banana, cut in ½-inch slices
2 tablespoons shredded coconut
½ cup macadamia nut bits,
  toasted
Whipped cream and whole
  macadamia nuts, for decoration

Combine the water, sugar and cinnamon stick in a medium-sized saucepan and bring to a boil. Reduce the heat and simmer, covered, for about 10 minutes. Remove from the heat, cool to room temperature and add the rum.

Combine the fruit and coconut in a large bowl. Pour the rum mixture over all. Cover, and chill for several hours. Stir in the macadamias and decorate with whipped cream and whole macadamias just before serving.

SERVES 4-6

Mango Cream

5 large ripe mangoes
Pinch of granulated sugar (to
  taste)
2 oranges, peeled and cut into
  small pieces
1 tablespoon lemon juice
2 cups heavy cream, whipped
1 cup macadamia nut bits
12 maraschino cherries
  (optional)

Puree the mangoes in a blender or food processor. Add sugar, orange pieces, lemon juice and whipped cream. Mix well. Fold in the nuts. Pile into tall parfait glasses. Chill. If desired, decorate with cherries before serving.

SERVES 12

Hot Apple Crunch

10 green cooking apples
2 cups flour
1 cup granulated sugar
1 teaspoon baking powder
1 egg
½ cup milk
8 tablespoons (1 stick) butter,
  softened
1 cup macadamia nut bits
2 tablespoons cinnamon sugar

Preheat the oven to 350 degrees. Grease and flour an 11-inch baking dish.

Pare the apples, then slice into bite-sized pieces. Arrange apples in the baking dish, forming an even layer. Combine the flour, sugar, baking powder, egg and milk in a large mixing bowl. Stir until the mixture is crumbly. Sprinkle evenly on top of the apples. Melt the butter in a saucepan over low heat and pour over the apples and flour mixture. Sprinkle the macadamia nut bits and cinnamon sugar.

Bake in the preheated oven for 45 minutes. Serve warm with whipped cream or French vanilla ice cream.

SERVES 10-12

Sugar Plum Pudding

¾ cup uncooked prunes, pitted
2 tablespoons orange juice
Grated rind of 1 orange
¾ cup flour
½ teaspoon baking powder
¼ teaspoon salt
1 teaspoon cinnamon
4 tablespoons (½ stick) butter,
  softened
½ cup light brown sugar, firmly
  packed
1 large egg
½ cup macadamia nut bits

Preheat the oven to 350 degrees. Grease and flour an 8-inch round cake pan.

Cut the prunes into small pieces. Mix with the orange juice and rind in a small bowl. Sift together the flour, baking powder, salt and cinnamon in another bowl. Cream the butter and sugar together in a mixing bowl until light and fluffy. Add the egg and beat well. Add the sifted flour mixture to the creamed mixture and blend until smooth. Stir in the prunes and orange juice, then the macadamias. Turn into the prepared pan.

Bake in the preheated oven for 30 to 35 minutes. Serve warm with vanilla ice cream.

SERVES 4

Mountains and Sea

✤ Cathy's Crepe Batter

2 eggs
1 teaspoon granulated sugar
1 tablespoon orange or almond
  liqueur
⅔ cup milk
½ teaspoon salt
1 cup flour
⅔ cup sparkling water
2 tablespoons butter, for
  cooking

Combine the eggs, sugar, liqueur, milk, salt and flour and mix well. Refrigerate for 1 hour. Stir in the sparkling water. Cook very thin crepes, using just enough butter for each to melt and cover the surface of the crepe pan.

MAKES 16 6-INCH CREPES

Macadamia Nut Filling

½ cup milk
¾ cup granulated sugar
1 tablespoon butter
2 cups ground macadamia nuts
½ teaspoon cinnamon
2 teaspoons rum
¾ cup fine breadcrumbs
Grated rind of 1 lemon

Scald the milk in a saucepan and stir in the sugar and butter. Combine the macadamias, cinnamon, rum, breadcrumbs and lemon rind in a mixing bowl, then add to the milk mixture and stir to mix well.

Place ¼ cup of filling on each crepe and roll into a cylinder. Cover with Mocha Sauce (below).

Mocha Sauce

1½ cups black coffee
6 ounces semisweet chocolate,
  cut in pieces
½ cup granulated sugar
3 tablespoons butter
2 tablespoons brandy

Heat the coffee and chocolate in a small, heavy saucepan. Add the sugar and butter and heat until smooth. Cool slightly and add the brandy. Serve warm on filled crepes.

MAKES FILLING AND SAUCE FOR 16 CREPES

✳ Linzertorte

16 tablespoons (2 sticks) butter,
  softened
1 cup granulated sugar
Grated rind of 1 orange
Grated rind of 1 lemon
2 egg yolks
1½ cups sifted flour
1 teaspoon baking powder
2 teaspoons cinnamon
½ teaspoon cloves
¼ teaspoon salt
1 cup ground macadamia nuts
1 cup tart fruit preserves
  (currant, plum or blackberry)

Preheat the oven to 350 degrees. Butter an 8-inch springform pan.

Cream the butter and sugar in a mixing bowl until fluffy. Add the grated citrus rinds and egg yolks, and beat well. Sift together the dry ingredients in a small bowl and blend into the creamed mixture. Stir in the nuts and work the dough with your hands until it is smooth. Chill for about 1 hour.

Press two-thirds of the chilled dough into the prepared pan, making an edge 1 inch high all around. Spread with three-fourths of the preserves. Form the remaining dough into long ½-inch-wide strips and lay these over the preserves in a lattice pattern. Use the remaining preserves to fill in the squares that are formed.

Bake in the preheated oven for 50 to 60 minutes, or until golden brown. Cool completely before cutting as a pie or in "squares," as desired.

SERVES 12-16

Chocolate Mousse

1 cup semisweet chocolate chips
3 tablespoons water
1 tablespoon brandy or rum
5 eggs at room temperature
Whipped cream and
  macadamia nut bits, for
  decoration

Melt the chocolate and water in a saucepan over low heat. Remove from the heat and stir in the brandy or rum. Separate the eggs. Beat the yolks well, then add to the chocolate mixture and beat until thick.

Beat the egg whites in a mixing bowl until peaks form. Pour the chocolate mixture into the whites and quickly fold together until just mixed. Spoon into serving bowls. Chill for at least 4 hours. Serve decorated with whipped cream and macadamias.

SERVES 4-6

✷✷ Macadamia Chocolate Mousse Pie

*Fine dry breadcrumbs, for
  dusting
8 ounces semisweet chocolate,
  cut into small pieces
¼ cup boiling water
8 eggs, separated
⅔ cup granulated sugar
4½ teaspoons rum
⅛ teaspoon salt
2 cups heavy cream
⅔ cup macadamia nut bits*

Preheat the oven to 350 degrees. Grease a 9-inch pie plate and dust with breadcrumbs.

Melt the chocolate and water in a small, heavy saucepan over low heat. Beat the egg yolks in the large bowl of an electric mixer at high speed for about 5 minutes, until thick and lemon-colored. Gradually beat in ⅓ cup sugar. Beat in the melted chocolate and stir in 1½ teaspoons of the rum.

Beat the egg whites and salt in another bowl until stiff peaks form. Stir a quarter of the egg whites into the chocolate mixture, then gently fold in the remaining whites. Fill the prepared pie plate to the top, using about 5 cups of the mixture. Cover and refrigerate the remainder.

Bake the pie in the preheated oven for 20 minutes, or until firm. Turn off the heat and leave the pie in the oven for 2 hours, then remove it and allow to cool on a rack for 2 more hours.

When the pie is completely cold, beat 1½ cups of the cream, ⅓ cup sugar and the remaining 3 teaspoons rum in a bowl until stiff. Fold into the reserved mousse and add all but 2 tablespoons of the macadamias. Spread this mixture on top of the pie. Beat the remaining ½ cup cream until stiff. Spoon onto the pie. Sprinkle with the remaining nuts. Chill the pie until ready to serve.

SERVES 6

✳ Rolled Macadamia Coconut Baklava

4 leaves strudel dough
8 tablespoons (1 stick) butter, melted
1 cup macadamia nut bits
1 cup shredded coconut
¼ cup granulated sugar
2 teaspoons cinnamon

Honey Syrup
½ cup water
¼ cup honey
½ cup granulated sugar
1 tablespoon lemon juice

Preheat the oven to 350 degrees. Have ready an ungreased cookie sheet.

Lay a leaf of strudel dough on a clean surface. Brush carefully with melted butter. Place a second leaf on top. Repeat the buttering/layering process with the remaining leaves.

To make the filling, combine the macadamias, coconut, sugar and cinnamon in a mixing bowl. Spread evenly on top of the layered strudel leaves, to within an inch of each edge. Roll up from the long side like a jelly roll, using a little melted butter to seal the edge, if necessary. Slice off the ragged ends, then slice the roll into 5 even cylinders. Stand the rolls on end on the cookie sheet. Pour 1 teaspoon melted butter over each.

Bake in the preheated oven for 10 minutes. Remove from the oven, turn the rolls over to stand on the other end, spoon again with melted butter, and return to the oven for 10 minutes more, or until golden brown.

Combine the ingredients for the honey syrup in a saucepan and bring to a boil over medium heat. Lower the heat and simmer for 10 minutes. Cool. Dip each hot roll in honey syrup and set on a wire rack above a pan to drip. Serve cold with a little extra syrup spooned over just before serving.

SERVES 5

✳ Ricotta-Macadamia Strudel

2 cups firm ricotta cheese
Grated rind and juice of
  1 lemon
¼ cup honey
2 eggs, beaten
½ teaspoon cinnamon
¼ teaspoon salt
⅓ cup macadamia nut bits
½ cup fine breadcrumbs
¼ cup golden raisins
8 tablespoons (1 stick) butter,
  melted
6 leaves strudel dough,
  unfrozen
½ cup wheat germ

Preheat the oven to 375 degrees. Grease a baking tray or cookie sheet.

To make the filling, combine the ricotta, lemon rind and juice, honey, eggs, cinnamon, salt, macadamias, breadcrumbs and raisins in a mixing bowl, and mix well.

Lay a leaf of strudel dough on a clean counter. Brush gently and generously with the melted butter and sprinkle with wheat germ. Place another strudel leaf on top, and repeat the process until all the leaves have been used.

Spread the filling on the strudel leaves on the end nearest you. Gently roll the dough away from you, tucking in the sides as you go. (Be careful not to roll too tightly as the strudel will expand in baking.) Carefully lift the roll onto the prepared baking sheet. Brush the top with melted butter. Make several diagonal slashes through the dough to the filling.

Bake in the preheated oven for 30 to 35 minutes, until golden and crisp. Cut gently with a serrated knife and serve either warm or cold.

Note: Cover the unbaked strudel leaves with a damp cloth until you are ready to use them.

SERVES 4-6

Canoes passing Mokuaikana church

✳ Lemon Soufflé

¾ cup granulated sugar
5 eggs, separated
Grated rind of 2 lemons
¼ cup lemon juice
½ cup ground macadamia nut
  bits

Preheat the oven to 350 degrees. Butter an 8-inch soufflé dish and dust with powdered sugar.

Beat the egg yolks in a mixing bowl until very light. Gradually add the sugar and beat until creamy. Add the lemon rind and juice and the macadamias. Beat the egg whites until stiff in another bowl. Fold lightly into the egg-yolk mixture and turn into the prepared dish.

Set the soufflé dish in a pan of hot water and bake in the preheated oven for 35 minutes, or until firm. Serve at once.

SERVES 4-6

✳ Maple Macadamia Soufflé

½ cup finely chopped
  macadamia nut bits
1½ teaspoons butter
2 tablespoons cornstarch
¾ cup whole milk
3 egg yolks, lightly beaten
½ teaspoon maple flavoring
4 egg whites
¼ teaspoon salt
⅛ teaspoon cream of tartar
½ cup sugar
¾ cup macadamia nut bits
Whipped cream, for decoration

Preheat the oven to 350 degrees. Have ready a 1-quart soufflé dish. Make a collar by cutting a piece of wax paper large enough to encircle the dish with a 2-inch overlap. Fold the paper in half lengthways. Grease the top third of the paper and the inside of the dish and sprinkle with macadamias. Tie the collar around the dish.

Melt the butter in a small, heavy saucepan over low heat. Remove from the heat and stir in the cornstarch, using a wire whisk. Gradually blend in the milk. Bring to a boil, stirring constantly, until the mixture thickens. Continue to cook over low heat for 2 minutes. Remove from the heat and use the whisk to beat the hot sauce into the beaten egg yolks. Stir in the maple flavoring.

Beat the egg whites with salt and cream of tartar in another bowl. Gradually beat in the sugar to form a thick, glossy meringue. Stir a quarter of the meringue into the egg-yolk mixture. Fold in the macadamias and the remaining meringue mixture. Turn into the prepared soufflé dish. If desired, sprinkle the top lightly with sugar.

Bake in the preheated oven for 50 to 55 minutes, or until well puffed and golden brown. Serve immediately, with whipped cream.

SERVES 4-6

✻ Date Soufflé

1 cup sliced dates
½ cup milk
2 tablespoons rum
2 tablespoons heavy cream
1 teaspoon vanilla extract
4 eggs, separated
½ cup sugar
½ cup macadamia nuts, ground
Confectioners' sugar (optional)

Preheat the oven to 350 degrees. Grease a 7-inch soufflé dish and sprinkle with sugar.

Combine the dates and milk in a saucepan and bring to a boil over medium-high heat. Cook about 10 minutes until the dates are soft. Remove from the heat and mash the dates to a paste. Beat in the rum, cream, vanilla and egg yolks. Whip the egg whites in another bowl until stiff peaks form, adding sugar gradually. Fold into the date mixture. Pour into the prepared soufflé dish and sprinkle the top with ground macadamias and a little confectioners' sugar, if desired.

Bake in the preheated oven for 40 to 45 minutes, or until puffed and lightly browned. Serve at once.

SERVES 4

✻ Prune Nut Soufflé

12 ounces pitted prunes
¼ teaspoon salt
1 tablespoon lemon juice
Grated rind of 1 lemon
¼ cup granulated sugar
½ cup macadamia nut bits
5 egg whites
Confectioners' sugar and
  whipped cream, for decoration

Put the prunes in a saucepan, cover with water and bring to a boil. Reduce the heat, cover and simmer for 25 minutes, or until the prunes are tender. Drain. Puree the prunes to measure 1 cup.

Preheat the oven to 350 degrees. Grease a 7-inch soufflé dish and dust with sugar.

Stir the salt, lemon juice and rind and sugar into the prune puree. Beat the egg whites in another bowl until stiff peaks form and fold them gently into the prune mixture. Turn into the prepared soufflé dish.

Bake in the preheated oven for 40 minutes, or until puffed and lightly browned. Sprinkle with confectioners' sugar and serve at once with whipped cream.

SERVES 4

Candies and Ice Cream

When people think of making candy or ice cream, they generally assume a lot of work is involved, but this is not always the case, as you will discover in the following selection of recipes. The spiced macadamia recipe is one of our favorites and requires surprisingly little time and just one saucepan! Even the fudge is not difficult if you use an accurate candy thermometer.

The most elaborate (and time-consuming) recipe is the Hawaiian Rainbow Bombe, which must be refrozen after each ice cream flavor is added. However, the mounting anticipation and the final festive appearance of the completed bombe add excitement to a special occasion.

A field of Orchids - to be used for leis or flower wreaths

Spiced Macadamias

1 cup granulated sugar
1 teaspoon cinnamon
Grated rind of 1 orange
⅛ teaspoon freshly grated
  nutmeg
½ cup milk
1 teaspoon butter
1 teaspoon vanilla extract
2 generous cups whole
  macadamia nuts
1-2 tablespoons orange juice

Combine the sugar, cinnamon, orange rind, nutmeg and milk in a heavy-bottomed saucepan. Cook until the mixture reaches the soft-ball stage (236 degrees on a candy thermometer). Remove from the heat and add the butter, vanilla and macadamias. Stir until the nuts are well coated. If the mixture turns dry, add 1 to 2 tablespoons orange juice and return to the heat until the desired consistency is reached.

Turn the nuts out onto wax paper, quickly separate them from one another and allow to dry.

MAKES 3 CUPS

✱ Macadamia Nougat

2 cups granulated sugar
1 teaspoon butter
2 cups macadamia nut bits

Grease a 9-inch square pan.

Put the sugar and butter into an iron skillet. Melt slowly over low heat, stirring constantly, until the sugar is a dark caramel. Immediately sprinkle in the macadamias, mix well and pour into the prepared pan. Cut at once into squares. Cool. Store in tightly closed containers.

MAKES 2 DOZEN

Macadamian Date Balls

1½ cups pitted dates, chopped
1 cup granulated sugar
¼ cup butter
1 egg, beaten
Pinch of salt
1 teaspoon vanilla extract
1½ cups Rice Krispies
¾ cup macadamia nut bits
6-ounce package shredded
  sweetened coconut

Cook the dates, sugar, butter, egg, salt and vanilla in a large saucepan over low heat for 10 minutes. While the mixture is still cooking, stir in the Rice Krispies and macadamias. Remove from the heat and cool slightly.

Form into balls, using buttered hands, and roll in the shredded coconut. Chill until ready to serve.

MAKES 3 DOZEN

✳ Creamy Nut Fudge

4 ounces baking chocolate, cut
  into small pieces
1¼ cups milk
3 cups granulated sugar
2 tablespoons light corn syrup
⅛ teaspoon salt
4 tablespoons (½ stick) butter
1 teaspoon vanilla extract
½ cup macadamia nut bits

Lightly grease an 8-inch square pan.

Put the chocolate and milk into a deep, heavy saucepan. Cook over low heat, stirring constantly, until the chocolate has melted. Stir in the sugar, corn syrup and salt. Cook, stirring occasionally, until the mixture reaches the soft-ball stage (236 degrees on a candy thermometer). Remove from the heat and stir in the butter. Cool at room temperature for about 1 hour, until the bottom of the saucepan feels only slightly warm. Add the vanilla and beat until the candy loses its gloss and starts to thicken. Quickly stir in the macadamias.

Pour into the prepared pan and cool until firm. Cut into squares.

MAKES 36

Macadamia Nut Clusters

4 ounces sweet cooking
  chocolate, broken into pieces
½ teaspoon vegetable shortening
¼ teaspoon cinnamon
¼ teaspoon nutmeg
¾ cup whole macadamia nuts

Line a cookie sheet with wax paper.

Put the chocolate in the top of a double boiler and melt over boiling water. Stir in the shortening, cinnamon and nutmeg until well blended and smooth. Stir in the macadamias until well coated. Remove from the heat.

Using two long-handled teaspoons, drop clusters of the mixture (with about 3 nuts in each cluster) onto the cookie sheet. Spoon any remaining chocolate over the clusters. Let stand in a cool place until the chocolate has set.

Remove the clusters from the cookie sheet with a spatula. Store in a covered container in a cool place.

MAKES 24

✶ Caramel Crunch Ice Cream

1½ cups milk
¾ cup granulated sugar, for
 caramel
⅛ teaspoon salt
3 egg yolks, beaten
⅓ cup granulated sugar
4 teaspoons very hot water
¾ cup macadamia nut bits
1 tablespoon vanilla extract
1 cup heavy cream
1 cup light cream

Scald the milk over low heat; do not boil. Stir in ¾ cup sugar and salt until dissolved. Put the beaten egg yolks in the top of a double boiler and slowly pour the hot milk over them. Beat until well blended. Cook over boiling water, stirring constantly, until lightly thickened. Cool and then chill for about 1 hour.

Meanwhile, caramelize ⅓ cup sugar in a heavy nonferrous pan. Melt the sugar over low heat, stirring constantly with a long-handled spoon, for about 10 minutes, until the sugar is straw-colored. Remove from the heat and *very slowly* add hot water. (If the water is added too suddenly, the caramel will pop in all directions, adding rather too much excitement to this recipe!) Return to the heat and stir in the macadamias. When the caramel and nuts form a ball, remove from the heat and cool slightly. Fold the vanilla, creams and the caramel-nut ball into the chilled custard. Allow the ball to harden and cool completely. Then remove from the custard and break into small pieces with your fingers. Return the bits to the custard and pour into the canister of an electric ice cream freezer.

Freeze as directed. Serve immediately or pack into airtight freezer containers to harden.

SERVES 5

Chocolate Candy Pie Crust

1 cup macadamia nut bits
2 ounces semisweet chocolate,
   cut in pieces
2 tablespoons butter
2 tablespoons milk
¾ cup confectioners' sugar,
   sifted

Lightly grease a 9-inch pie pan.

Combine the chocolate, butter and milk in a medium-sized, heavy saucepan and stir constantly over low heat until the chocolate melts. Remove from the heat. Stir in the confectioners' sugar and macadamias. Press onto the bottom and sides of the prepared pie pan. Refrigerate until set, and fill with Mint Ice Cream (below).

Mint Ice Cream

1 pint good-quality vanilla ice
   cream (homemade is best, of
   course)
2-4 tablespoons green creme de
   menthe, to taste
Whole macadamia nuts, for
   decoration

Stir the ice cream until slightly softened. Fold in the creme de menthe. Turn into the pie shell. Top with a whole macadamia nut per serving. Freeze.

SERVES 6-8

Note: Substitute coffee ice cream for vanilla and Kahlua for creme de menthe to make a different but equally delicious frozen dessert.

Skip's Macadamia Ice Cream Sauce

½ cup granulated sugar
½ cup light corn syrup
½ teaspoon salt
1 cup macadamia nut bits,
   ground to a paste
½ teaspoon vanilla extract

Put the sugar, corn syrup and salt in a heavy saucepan and bring to a boil over medium heat. Simmer until all the sugar crystals have dissolved. Turn off the heat and immediately stir in the macadamia paste and vanilla.

Serve warm over ice cream. To store, cool and keep refrigerated in a tightly covered container.

MAKES 1½ CUPS

✤ ✤ Hawaiian Rainbow Bombe

½ gallon raspberry sherbet
1 pint coffee ice cream
2 tablespoons rum
¾ cup macadamia nut bits
1 quart vanilla ice cream
1 pint strawberry ice cream
1 pint lime sherbet

Begin preparation of this dessert a day ahead!

Lightly butter the inside of a small, 8-by-4-inch ice cream mold. Stir the raspberry sherbet until softened *just* enough to spread; coat the entire top of the mold about ½ inch thick. (You may need to use your fingers to get it even.) Reserve 1 cup of the sherbet. Freeze for 2 hours or more, until that layer is set.

Repeat the process for the coffee ice cream, spreading it about ¼ inch thick and refreezing until set.

Stir the rum and macadamias into slightly softened vanilla ice cream and spread this an inch thick or more. Refreeze. Next add a ½-inch layer of strawberry ice cream, then a 1-inch layer of lime sherbet, and finally fill the center with the remaining raspberry sherbet. Refreeze between each step, and finally return the mold to the freezer for at least 2 hours, preferably overnight. Freeze well.

To unmold, set the mold briefly in a large bowl of hot water, or run it quickly under hot tap water. Slice and serve immediately.

SERVES 8-10

Note: The quantities of ice cream needed will vary according to mold sizes. Please feel free to design your own bombes.